UP YOUR SERVICE!

"Ron Kaufman is an unending spring of creative, effective ideas for delivering quality service. His commitment and enthusiasm are contagious. *Read and use this book!*"

Richard Farrell
Director of Customer Service, **Alibris**
"Books you thought you'd never find" www.alibris.com

"If you've seen Ron Kaufman LIVE you know what *energy* is on stage. Now you hold hundreds of winning ideas and Ron's powerful enthusiasm right in your hands. Let this book take you and your organization straight to the top."

Robin A. Speculand
Vice President, Quality & Service
Citibank

"Read this book before your competitors do! And then give it to all your managers to read. Every chapter is loaded with enough common sense and good ideas to pay you back 1,000 times."

Todd Lapidus
President
Customer Contact Corporation

"Ron Kaufman is passionate about partnerships and service. He has a keen eye for detail and an extraordinary knack for revealing strategic implications. Ron's straight-to-the-point insights and recommendations are meaningful and valuable for organizations that are serious about making a positive change."

Nolan Tan
Chief Executive Officer
The Service Quality Centre

"Ron Kaufman writes like he teaches. *UP Your Service!* is fast-paced, upbeat and action-oriented for easy translation from concepts to useful application.

It is sprinkled with relevant examples of service we encounter in our everyday lives with firms we know – some only too well!

This book contains a generous dose of Ron's humorous yet impactful approach. Like attending one of Ron's presentations, it makes you want to get up immediately and do something about improving the service level you and your company provide.

Knowing Ron, he will not be satisfied if you only read this book. He'll want to see you out there actually *"Upping Your Service!""*

Sim Kay Wee
Senior Vice President, Cabin Crew
Singapore Airlines

"No one knows more about service – and delighting customers – than Ron Kaufman. If you're a business professional and want to remain not just relevant but important in the new economy, you need to read this book and apply what you learn right away."

Michael Alan Hamlin
Managing Director, **TeamAsia**
Author, *The New Asian Corporation*

"*UP Your Service!* is fun and useful – very much like Ron Kaufman – making service quality a subject relevant for everyone. This book is a master manual of the do's and don'ts in service. Do get the book. Don't put it down!"

Tan Chin Tiong, PhD
Provost
Singapore Management University

"*UP Your Service!* is a must-have for every company and everybody. In these pages you will find the most effective service solutions and many treasured gems. This book is a global benchmark and a milestone for quality customer service."

David Hall
Director, New Business Development
The Home Shopping Network

"Ron Kaufman is a practical philosopher of customer service. He gives you a map you can follow with your head and your heart. Ron's practical strategies show how to generate superb service as an individual, a team or a company. The name of the game today is service. Ron Kaufman can help us all win."

Philip Hallstein
Executive Vice President, Customer Satisfaction
SportsMind

"Ron Kaufman, whom I am proud and privileged to call a friend, is dedicated to serving humanity. He knows that the golden road to success lies through making people happy. Let him help make you happy and successful, too. *Read this wonderful book!*"

Ashleigh Brilliant
Creator of **POT-SHOTS**
Author, *I May Not Be Perfect, But Parts Of Me Are Excellent*

"When Ron was little we called him *the lovin' oven* because he emanated so much goodwill. He hasn't changed one bit! *UP Your Service!* has that same positive energy. Let Ron inspire you to give service that comes from your heart."

Ruth H. Kaufman
Ron's **Mother**

YOUR SERVICE!

Strategies and Action Steps to
Delight Your Customers NOW!

Ron Kaufman

www.RonKaufman.com

Published by Ron Kaufman Pte Ltd. - 10 9 8 7 6
The moral right of the author has been asserted.
UP Your Service! is a registered trademark of Ron Kaufman Pte Ltd.

Cover photographs and photo on page 167 by Munshi Ahmed.
Typography, interior photography and design by Pagesetters Pte Ltd.
Page layout by Jidi Ng. Edited by Brendan Atkins.
Set in Palatino with Helvetica accents. Printed in Singapore.

UP Your Service! *Strategies and Action Steps to Delight Your Customers NOW!*
ISBN 981-04-2132-X   320 pages, includes index.

1. Customer Service	2. Marketing and Sales	3. Management
4. Self-improvement	5. Ron Kaufman	6. Title

Permissions:

Raffles Hotel doorman, Mr. Sarjit Singh, appears on page 167 courtesy of Raffles
International.

Miss Brighten Sabriya Kaufman appears on pages 127 and 231 with permission
of her mother.

All quotations are attributed as known. Those not otherwise indicated are by the author.

ATTENTION: Customer Service and Training Managers

Special purchases for your service team:

Special discounts are available for volume purchases of this book
for in-house training programs, sales promotions, staff and
customer premiums and special conference events.

For more information, contact:

Ron Kaufman Pte Ltd, 50 Bayshore Park #31-01, Aquamarine
Tower, Singapore 469977   Fax: (+65) 6444-8292
e-mail: reprints@RonKaufman.com
Website: http://www.RonKaufman.com

SERVICE

*IS THE CURRENCY THAT KEEPS
THE ECONOMY MOVING.*

*I SERVE YOU IN ONE BUSINESS,
YOU SERVE ME IN ANOTHER.*

*WHEN EITHER OF US IMPROVES,
THE ECONOMY GETS A LITTLE BETTER.*

*WHEN BOTH OF US IMPROVE,
PEOPLE ARE SURE TO NOTICE.*

*WHEN EVERYONE IMPROVES,
THE WHOLE WORLD GROWS
STRONGER AND CLOSER TOGETHER.*

RON KAUFMAN

The way I see it...

Life on this spinning Earth is an extraordinary and magnificent adventure. We come to the whole experience naked, wet and rather unprepared. Other people take care of us; they feed, bathe, clothe, educate and nurture us through the early years. They *serve* us. And we grow.

Gradually we develop skills, preferences and a personality. In our professional, personal and family lives, we learn how to give something back. We discover what it means (and how it feels) to be generous, add value, demonstrate concern for others. We learn how to show respect and how to earn it. We learn to be in *service*.

As our lives unfold, no one knows for sure what lies ahead: opportunities, challenges, good fortune, sometimes danger.

You want the best for you and yours. I want the best for mine.

We seek goodness for our family members, kindness for the old and young, understanding and compassion when in need. We want celebration when we're on a high, and commiseration when we're low. We want people in our lives who'll lend a hand, give a damn, pass a compliment, share a smile, willingly go the extra mile.

You've heard the phrase: *"What goes around, comes around."* Well, I believe it's true. Let's make our dance upon this Earth the best that it can be. It's up to us *together* now. Life responds to you and me.

Ron Kaufman
Singapore, 2002

What's going UP?

Quality service, excellent service, world-class, tip-top, red-carpet service. Impeccable, unbelievable, spectacular service.

Everyone is talking about SERVICE.

Here's why!

Delighted customers are more loyal, come more often, spend more money and tell their friends about you.

That means more pleasure and more profits for you.

Angry customers leave in a hurry, cancel orders, upset your staff and tell negative stories about you.

The benefits of *your* service going UP are clear. But *how* do you make it happen?

This fun-to-read, easy-to-use book shows you clearly what to do, plus how to do it – and why: proven strategies and practical action steps to successfully *UP Your Service!*

Get ready for a challenging and rewarding ride, packed with high-value learning and hundreds of new ideas.

Now turn the page. Let's work together to get your service going *UP!*

Get a FREE Service Newsletter!

Now you can receive Ron Kaufman's *free* monthly newsletter, *'The Best of Active Learning'*. It's packed with real stories and good ideas – including key learning points and practical action steps to boost your service, partnerships and culture.

To get your free subscription, send any e-mail message to: **join-bestof@RonKaufman.com**

Thank you all!

This book began in 1990 when I helped create and launch the Service Quality Centre in Singapore. Mr. Sim Kay Wee, Senior Vice President of Singapore Airlines and the original Chairman of the SQCentre, inspired me to blaze an enthusiastic path to help people everywhere *UP Your Service!*

Over the years, many clients have granted me the privilege of working with their teams and their ambitions. My style is to educate and encourage, but also to challenge and provoke. In this pursuit, I could not ask for better people to work with, and learn with, over the years. Thank you for all the speeches, workshops, conferences, retreats and teambuilding events we have created together. In the crucible of our co-invention the ideas in this book were tried and tested – and proven strong.

I have tried to keep **you** foremost in my mind. You the reader. You the service provider. You the person who can make a difference in the lives of many others. May *UP Your Service!* bring you ideas you can apply, references you recognize and examples you will enjoy.

And if you smile from time to time at the photos in the text, that's a delightful bonus.

May this book, and your daily actions, make our world a better place to live and learn, to love and serve and grow.

Table of Contents

Preface
Acknowledgments
Use this book to your advantage

CHAPTER 1

UP Your Service! Why Bother?   1

What's in it for your customers? · What's in it for you? · A vicious slide downwards into doom · A victorious ride upwards to success! · Climbing the ladder of customer loyalty · Look who's standing on the ladder! · Customer expectations are going *UP!* · Who deserves great service? · I Serve, You Serve · What would *you* do? · *UP Your Service!* action steps

CHAPTER 2

It takes an *UP Your Service!* Mindset   17

Abundant generosity · Genuine compassion · The *'can-do'* spirit! · Eagerness to learn and grow · Take personal responsibility · See the world from your customer's point of view · We become what we think about · What would *you* do? · *UP Your Service!* action steps

CHAPTER 3

It takes an *UP Your Service!* Toolset   29

Excellent products and services · Efficient delivery systems · Competent, well-trained people · User-friendly policies and procedures · Customer information database · Comprehensive feedback systems · A system for continuous improvement · Effective organizational structure · Keep your toolset up-to-date! · What would *you* do? · *UP Your Service!* action steps

CHAPTER 4

It takes an *UP Your Service!* Culture   **43**

Your service philosophy · New staff recruitment · New staff orientation · Training and development · Rewards and recognition · Appraisal and promotions · Company social events · Internal communications · Management and staff interaction · Physical atmosphere and ambience · Rites, rituals and traditions · Staff suggestion schemes · Community relations · Management role modeling · The question of *empowerment* · When culture nourishes, service flourishes · How do you get more bananas? · What would *you* do? · *UP Your Service!* action steps

CHAPTER 5

UP Your Service! Standards   **71**

Criminal belongs in jail! · Basic is the bare minimum · Expected is just the average · Desired is what people hope for! · Surprising is leading the field! · Unbelievable is truly world class! · Where are *you* and *your company* today? · Where are *your competitors* today? · What would *you* do? · *UP Your Service!* action steps

CHAPTER 6

UP Your Service! Interactions   **89**

The one-shot deal · Transaction satisfaction · Reliable relationships · Powerful partnerships · More examples of service interactions · Which interactions are *you* doing? · What would *you* do? · *UP Your Service!* action steps

CHAPTER 7

Explore, Agree, Deliver, Assure   **99**

Understand each other: *explore* · Make clear promises: *agree* · Do what you promised: *deliver* · Confirm satisfaction: *assure* · How thoroughly do you *explore*? · How readily do you *agree*? · How consistently do you *deliver* · How completely do you *assure*? · Benchmarking Amazon.com · How does Amazon.com do it? · Planning your wedding · Upgrading a computer network · Buying insurance · Selling insurance · Hiring new team members · Building trust is a four-step process · What would *you* do? · *UP Your Service!* action steps

CHAPTER 8

Understanding Perception Points 117

Perception points are all around · Tune in to your senses · Perception points in the service cycle · Perception points on an airline · Perception points at a website · Perception points with a courier service · Perception points from the *pediatric dentist's* point of view · Perception points from the *young patient's* point of view · Perception points on a date · Identify *your* perception points · What would *you* do? · *UP Your Service!* action steps

CHAPTER 9

Understanding Value Dimensions 133

Some like it hard... and some like it softer · Same *service*, many different values · Same *product*, many different values · Common value dimensions · Want to add more *value*? Be sure you know *which* value to add! · The ultimate value dimension · Different *values* all around the cycle · What do *your* customers value most? · What would *you* do? · *UP Your Service!* action steps

CHAPTER 10

How to Get Close to Your Customers 147

Do you really know your customers? · Conduct surveys · Set up a customer hotline · Visit your customer's site · Invite your customers to visit you · Hire a mystery shopper · Shop your competition · Study complaints...and compliments · Focusing with focus groups · Benchmark inside and out · What would *you* do? · *UP Your Service!* action steps

CHAPTER 11

Craft Your Service Vision 163

Call it what you will! · What turns your customers *on?* · What turns your people *on?* · The Raffles Hotel mission statement · Your vision might be a moving target · Keep these points in mind · Who is your service vision for? · Make your vision a challenge to all · Use this worksheet · Write your new service vision here · What would *you* do? · *UP Your Service!* action steps

CHAPTER 12

Polish Your Perception Points 175

Polish your *people* · Polish your *product* · Polish your *packaging* · Polish your *policies* and *procedures* · Polish what can be *seen* · Polish what can be *heard* · Polish what can be *touched* · Polish what can be *smelled* and *tasted* · How *fast* is this line moving? · Put your best foot forward · Even the tax collector has a perception point or two · Do you feel the need for speed? · Leave a good impression when you go · What would *you* do? · *UP Your Service!* action steps

CHAPTER 13

Make Your Customers Information Rich! 191

What makes the difference? *Information!* · Overwhelmed and overloaded is *not* the same as *rich!* · *Who* should be information rich? · *What* makes people information rich? · *When* to make people information rich · *Where* to provide rich information · *How* to make people information rich · *Why* make people information rich? · What would *you* do? · *UP Your Service!* action steps

CHAPTER 14

Cultivate Customer Contact 207

Cultivate contact *face-to-face* · Cultivate contact with *body language* · Cultivate contact on the *telephone* · Cultivate contact with *voicemail* · Cultivate contact in *writing* · Write compliments to encourage · Write complaints that carry clout! · Cultivate contact using *e-mail* · Cultivate contact at your *website* · What would *you* do? · *UP Your Service!* action steps

CHAPTER 15

Bounce Back with *UP Your Service!* Recovery 225

Problems can be *good* for you! · Make it *easy* for customers to complain · Who bothers to complain? · When things go wrong, use S.E.R.V.I.C.E · They bounced back! · How generous should you be? · What is the lifetime value of a customer? · When your customer is ready to *explode!* · Bounce back by *writing* back · How to make a *wrong* customer feel *right* · Your service was inefficient! · Your staff were so rude! · Managing customer expectations · Build a *culture* for service recovery · What would *you* do? · *UP Your Service!* action steps

CHAPTER 16

UP Your Service! Guaranteed!   247

What is an *UP Your Service!* guarantee? · What are the *benefits* of a service guarantee for your *customers?* · What are the *benefits* of a service guarantee for your *employees?* · What are the *benefits* of a service guarantee for your *organization?* · What a service guarantee *cannot* do · Sixteen steps to launch your guarantee · *When* should you launch your guarantee? · What would *you* do? · *UP Your Service!* action steps

CHAPTER 17

UP Your Service! Integration and Innovation   259

Merge two or more fields · Integrating for customers on the inside…and on the outside · Turn negatives into positives! · Leverage any value dimension · What would *you* do? · *UP Your Service!* action steps

CHAPTER 18

Keeping Track of Service   267

Measurements can be complex · Measurements can be straightforward · Track customer expectations · Track customer perceptions · Track customer preferences · Track competitive position · Who are you going to ask? · What would *you* do? · *UP Your Service!* action steps

CHAPTER 19

What Wise People Say About Service   275

What do *you* have to say about service?

CHAPTER 20

Inspired Acts of Service   285

Brighten up those around you · Organ donation is a final act of service

Index   288

Use this book to your advantage

UP Your Service! will boost your spirit, build your business and help enrich your life.

Step by action step

Read two pages a day, a chapter each week, or the entire book in an action-packed month. *Apply what you learn right away.*

Work with your team-mates

Take *UP Your Service!* to work. Share it with your colleagues. Choose the best ideas and put them to work together.

Engage your suppliers

Ask your suppliers to improve the service they give *you*. After all, you are their customer in an interconnected chain. If you *get* better service from them, you'll be able to *give* better service to your customers, too. *(Giving them a copy of this book will help!)*

Inform your customers

Let customers know you are working to *UP Your Service!* Explain your action plans and welcome their suggestions. Customers will appreciate your efforts and applaud your improved results.

Share with those you love

UP Your Service! with your friends and family members. This positive, generous approach can enrich every aspect of your life.

Visit the website

www.RonKaufman.com is packed with articles, newsletters, audio, video and live event photographs and more. Visit today.

1

UP Your Service!
Why bother?

To get your service UP! takes a lot of time and effort.
Is it all worthwhile?

After all, customers can be cranky and unreasonable,
occasionally a 'pain in the neck'.

Colleagues and bosses can have a bad day, or a bad week.
And take it all out on you.

Your suppliers might be late, make a mistake
or forget about your order altogether.

You could wake up one morning looking for a break,
rather than another service challenge.

Maybe you will throw up your hands and say,
"UP My Service? Why bother?"

Good question!
(The answer is every bit as important.)

*This chapter explains why **you must** make the effort*
*to successfully **UP Your Service!***

What's in it for your customers?

When you *UP Your Service!* for customers, they get a lot!

- *Better service* means customers receive greater *value* from each of their purchase decisions.

- People don't just buy products. They ask for help when making decisions, require support during installation, need training to maximize usage and expect reassurance if things go wrong. These service 'extras' are important: they yield genuine customer *value*.

- *Quality service* provides customers with an enjoyable and emotionally rewarding experience. It makes people *feel good* about themselves and their decision to do business with you.

- Customers who receive *excellent service* feel positive and secure about their choices. In a world filled with complaints and complications, people remember the times when *"I made the right decision."*

- *Superior service* lets customers face the future with confidence, knowing that questions and problems will be handled in a professional way.

- *Red-carpet service* expands your customer's network of trusted service providers.

Your Customers

Have you ever recommended a store or a good restaurant to a friend, and said, *"Be sure to tell them that I sent you!"*?

Why do you do that?

Because you want your friends to enjoy the same quality of service you receive. And you want the positive reputation of the restaurant to reflect right back on you.

- *World-class service* gives your customers special 'bragging rights', something unique and desirable to talk about with their friends, family and neighbors.

Complaints spread quickly through gossip and idle chatter. But who wants to listen to a complainer? Stories of *winning service* make pleasant conversation for everyone, reflecting a glow of good feelings back to the story-teller.

- Finally, *UP Your Service!* boosts the self-esteem of customers and service providers alike. Everyone will want to work more effectively, think more creatively and behave more generously towards others.

Take this *UP Your Service!* quiz

How do customers feel, and what do they say, about you?

Yes / No	Our customers *feel good* about doing business with us.
Yes / No	Our customers tell us *"I made the right decision to work or shop with you."*
Yes / No	Customers talk positively about us to their friends and colleagues.
Yes / No	We get plenty of referrals from our existing customers.
Yes / No	Our staff feel great about the level of service we provide.

What's in it for you?

UP Your Service! also has tremendous benefits for you and your team of committed service providers.

- *Impeccable service* creates delighted customers, which leads to more business, increased sales, added revenue and higher profits. *UP Your Service!* makes you more successful.

- *Unbelievable service* creates loyal and committed customers. This benefits **you** in four specific ways:

  1. Loyal customers come back to buy more from you more often. They are also most likely to purchase your newest services and premium products.

  2. Loyal customers recommend you to others, spreading *positive word of mouth* in person, and *positive word of mouse* through e-mail and postings on the Internet.

  3. Loyal customers tend to be more understanding and forgiving when things go wrong.

  4. In fact, loyal customers make an effort to help you improve. They let you know where your products or processes may be weak, and what you need to do to stay one step ahead of your competition.

- *Leading-edge service* earns you and your organization a positive reputation. It gives you prestige in your industry and your community. It raises your profile, enhances your image, brings you recognition, admiration, and sometimes even fame.

- Finally, *UP Your Service!* enthuses people and makes them glad to be working together. It conveys and creates personal satisfaction. It's a winning result for everyone: customers, colleagues, prospects, suppliers *and you!*

Take this *UP Your Service!* quiz

How do you feel about the service you provide?

Yes / No   I am pleased with the service level we provide to our customers.

Yes / No   When I meet new people, I am proud to tell them what I do and where I work.

Yes / No   I am confident that customers will receive winning service from my organization, regardless of whether they are served by me or my colleagues.

Yes / No   If a customer has a problem with my company, I know we will do whatever necessary to set things right.

Yes / No   My company is continually working to improve the level of service we provide.

Yes / No   My company welcomes customer feedback. Complaints and compliments are highly valued.

Yes / No   Our commitment to winning service is included in our vision, mission statement, core values, recruitment, orientation, appraisals, rewards and recognition programs.

A vicious slide downwards into doom

Poor service to customers…leads to…

Upset customers…leads to…

Negative word of mouth…leads to…

A lousy reputation…leads to…

Fewer customers (who never come back!)…
leads to…

Lower profits…leads to…

Reduced income for employees…leads to…

Frustrated managers…leads to…

Unhappy staff…leads to…

Poor service…leads to…

Lousy service <u>undermines</u> great product

I visited an expensive restaurant with my wife. We found a terrific menu, fabulous food, elegant atmosphere and great music.

But the waiter was atrocious. He avoided our table when we needed help and stayed much too close when we wanted a private moment. He confused our orders, forgot my change, spilled a drink and never cracked a smile.

Maybe he just had a bad night. But he spoiled our evening, too.

The restaurant 'product' was great, it's true, but we haven't gone back since. And that was years ago! Poor quality service destroyed our memory of the evening and spoiled our appetites at that restaurant forever. We have no desire to return.

A victorious ride upwards to success!

Great service...leads to...

Enthusiastic staff...leads to...

Motivated managers...leads to...

Higher income for employees...leads to...

Higher profits...leads to...

More customers (who keep coming back!)... leads to...

An excellent reputation...leads to...

Positive word of mouth...leads to...

Delighted customers...leads to...

Great service to customers...leads to...

Winning service <u>overcomes</u> weak product

I had lunch with a client at a sandwich shop nearby. He ordered the tuna salad sandwich. I had the vegetarian deluxe.

After we started to eat, the friendly waiter stopped by to check on our meals. I sent compliments to the chef for my delicious lunch. My client did not complain, but he did not compliment, either.

The attentive waiter noticed. Without prompting, he offered to exchange the tuna salad sandwich for anything else on the menu. Grateful, my client chose another item.

I have returned to this sandwich shop many times. And I always tip the waiters. The quality of service is great. (Can't say the same about the tuna salad sandwich!)

Climbing the ladder of customer loyalty

"Here you win!"

The Ambassador
will work to promote you.

The Advocate
will tell others about you.

The Loyal Customer
wants to keep working with you.

The Acquaintance
has heard a bit
about you.

"Here you start!"

The Stranger
doesn't know you.

The Disappointed
will avoid
you.

"Here you lose!"

The Angry Customer
will speak negatively
to others about you.

The Terrorist
truly wants to hurt you.

Look who's standing on the ladder!

The Ambassador actively promotes you, writes to the local paper, makes introductions, gives recommendations, passes on your business card, encourages others to work with you. This partner says, *"Let's invent a future together."*

The Advocate mentions you positively to friends and colleagues, will write a testimonial letter if asked, is ready to endorse you sincerely to others. This admirer says, *"I insist on doing my business with you."*

The Loyal Customer returns to you again and again, buys your latest products, is willing to pay a little more, gives you suggestions to improve and is not easily swayed away by offers from your competition. This supporter says, *"I prefer continuing my relationship with you."*

The Acquaintance has heard about you but has no strong opinion. They may do business with you if your offer is good, but may just as easily go to your competition. This prospect says, *"I am aware of you. I know you exist."*

The Stranger has no idea who you are and has no opinion about you. This person says, *"I don't know what makes you different from everyone else."*

The Disappointed has no intention of working with you again. This upset customer says, *"I don't trust you. I don't want to do business with you any more."*

The Angry Customer had a bad experience in the past and now actively rejects you. This disgruntled person says, *"You have harmed me. You owe me more than just compensation."*

The Terrorist is committed to damaging your reputation. This disdainful protestor says, *"I seek revenge! I will discourage others from doing anything positive with you."*

Customer expectations are going *UP!*

Customers expect more than ever before: more quality, more features, more benefits, more variety, more flexibility, more value. And now they want *more service*.

Look at the trend in computers. Years ago, customers cared about the availability and reliability of their machines. Was the computer working? Had the system crashed? Did the software freeze? Was the printer jammed...*again?*

As technical issues were resolved, expectations grew. Customers bought computers that were faster, smaller and cheaper. Lighter machines with larger hard drives. Smaller footprints with bigger screens. Shorter access times and longer battery life.

Now computers have all the bells and whistles. And what do customers want today? *MORE SERVICE.*

Today, leading companies like **Dell Computer** provide:
- easy-to-use ordering systems on the telephone and the Web
- expert advice on hardware and software topics
- on-site repair, 'Next Day, Desk Side, 24 Hours Guaranteed'
- telephone support without spending all day on hold
- on-line technical assistance with rapid reply by e-mail
- a self-service website with helpful FAQs, easy-to-download software upgrades, user-to-user discussion groups and more.

Take a look at the airlines. It used to be a safe journey and an in-flight magazine were all that customers expected. Then airlines began to compete on the size and shape of adjustable seats, award-winning food and wines, telephones, fax machines, computer games and even gambling in the skies.

Today, most airlines provide newspapers, magazines, audio and video selections, up-to-date news and entertainment, duty-free shopping, laptop power points and frequent flyer awards. Some even feature reclining beds with custom-made pajamas!

With so much comfort and equipment, competition is intense. And what do customers want? *MORE SERVICE.*

The top airlines now remember who you are, where you live and all your contact numbers. They automatically book your favorite seat and your choice of meals.

Winning airlines of the future will go even further. Check-in agents and cabin crew will see your digital photo on computer screens prior to your arrival. They will recognize you instantly and welcome you by name. Your preferences for special service will be recorded during the journey and then carried forward to assist the crew on future flights.

"Welcome aboard again, Mr. Kaufman. Would you like the Wall Street Journal and a tomato juice with extra lime before take-off?"

Your personal interests will be matched with special offers.

"Hello Mr. Kaufman. We are arranging a group vacation to one of our most popular destinations, exclusively for vegetarian scuba divers with young children. Would you be interested in knowing more?"

UP Your Service! knows no bounds. In Switzerland, passengers wear heavy overcoats to the airport during winter months. But what if their destination is a tropical island like Bermuda or Singapore? Who needs a heavy overcoat near the equator?

Swissair will store your overcoat in their First Class lounge at the airport and have it waiting to warm you up the moment you return. Other airlines flying to Europe have had the same idea, but have not put it into action. Good ideas alone don't count. Implementation is what makes the difference!

Let's take this service even higher. When you leave your overcoat at the First Class lounge, would you like the airline to arrange for dry-cleaning while you are out of town?

That's customer expectations *and* customer service…*going UP!*

Who deserves great service?

UP Your Service! to channel partners and resellers. They will pass it on to your 'end customers'. Provide up-to-date information, reliable delivery, effective training and favorable terms.

UP Your Service! is a two-way street. Become a 'preferred customer' with suppliers. Appreciate their people and products. Work smoothly with their systems. Give them ideas to improve.

Distributors & Channel Partners

Vendors & Suppliers

UP Your Service! to your customers and you will reap the rewards of high

You can even get *UP!* with the government. Complete filings and

Your Customers

Government Agencies

praise, high profits, personal satisfaction, community respect and a sterling professional reputation.

applications on time. Provide constructive feedback. Compliment informed and helpful staff.

Family Members

Friends & Colleagues

Winning with your family is a foundation for success in other areas of your life. Give yours the attention and special service they deserve. Praise parents. Encourage children. Cherish your partner or spouse. Make family time a winning time for everyone…including you!

These are the people who help you out, perk you up and cheer you on. Be sure to return the favor! Be there when they need a hand, a friendly ear, or a shoulder to cry on. Send postcards, remember birthdays, pass along articles, websites and referrals. And celebrate their successes as they encourage yours.

We live in a constellation of relationships based upon *service*.

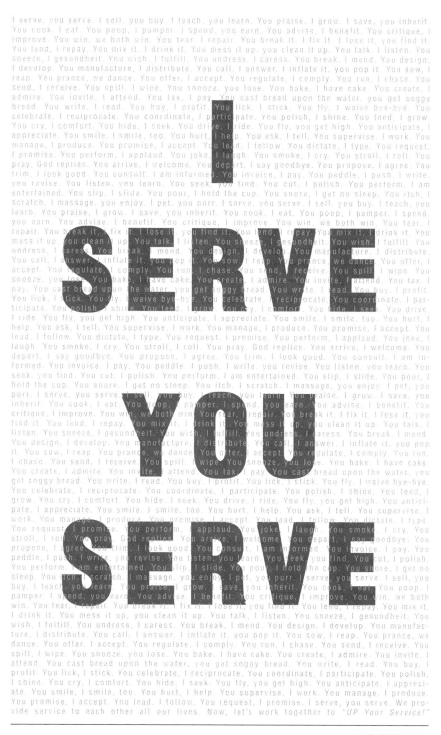

I serve, you serve. I sell, you buy. I teach, you learn. You praise, I grow. I save, you inherit. You cook, I eat. You poop, I pamper. I spend, you earn. You advise, I benefit. You critique, I improve. You win, we both win. You tear, I repair. You break it, I fix it. I lose it, you find it. You lend, I repay. You mix it. I drink it. You mess it up, you clean it up. You talk, I listen. You sneeze, I gesundheit. You wish, I fulfill. You undress, I caress. You break, I mend. You design, I develop. You manufacture, I distribute. You call, I answer. I inflate it, you pop it. You sow, I reap. You prance, we dance. You offer, I accept. You regulate, I comply. You run, I chase. You send, I receive. You spill, I wipe. You snooze, you lose. You bake, I have cake. You create, I admire. You invite, I attend. You tax, I pay. You cast bread upon the water, you get soggy bread. You write, I read. You buy, I profit. You lick, I stick. You fly, I waive bye-bye. You celebrate, I reciprocate. You coordinate, I participate. You polish, I shine. You feed, I grow. You cry, I comfort. You hide, I seek. You drive, I ride. You fly, you get high. You anticipate, I appreciate. You smile, I smile, too. You hurt, I help. You ask, I tell. You supervise, I work. You manage, I produce. You promise, I accept. You lead, I follow. You dictate, I type. You request, I promise. You perform, I applaud. You joke, I laugh. You smoke, I cry. You stroll, I roll. You pray, God replies. You arrive, I welcome. You depart, I say goodbye. You propose, I agree. You trim, I look good. You consult, I am informed. You invoice, I pay. You peddle, I push. I write, you revise. You listen, you learn. You seek, you find. You cut, I polish. You perform, I am entertained. You slip, I slide. You pour, I hold the cup. You snore, I get no sleep. You itch, I scratch. I massage, you enjoy. I pet, you purr. I serva, you serve. I sell, you buy. I teach, you learn. You praise, I grow. I save, you inherit. You cook, I eat. You poop, I pamper. I spend, you earn. You advise, I benefit. You critique, I improve. You win, we both win. You tear, I repair. You break it, I fix it. I lose it, you find it. You lend, I repay. You mix it. I drink it. You mess it up, you clean it up. You talk, I listen. You sneeze, I gesundheit. You wish, I fulfill. You undress, I caress. You break, I mend. You design, I develop. You manufacture, I distribute. You call, I answer. I inflate it, you pop it. You sow, I reap. You prance, we dance. You offer, I accept. You regulate, I comply. You run, I chase. You send, I receive. You spill, I wipe. You snooze, you lose. You bake, I have cake. You create, I admire. You invite, I attend. You tax, I pay. You cast bread upon the water, you get soggy bread. You write, I read. You buy, I profit. You lick, I stick. You fly, I waive bye-bye. You celebrate, I reciprocate. You coordinate, I participate. You polish, I shine. You feed, I grow. You cry, I comfort. You hide, I seek. You drive, I ride. You fly, you get high. You anticipate, I appreciate. You smile, I smile, too. You hurt, I help. You ask, I tell. You supervise, I work. You manage, I produce. You promise, I accept. You lead, I follow. You dictate, I type. You request, I promise. You perform, I applaud. You joke, I laugh. You smoke, I cry. You stroll, I roll. You pray, God replies. You arrive, I welcome. You depart, I say goodbye. You propose, I agree. You trim, I look good. You consult, I am informed. You invoice, I pay. You peddle, I push. I write, you revise. You listen, you learn. You seek, you find. You cut, I polish. You perform, I am entertained. You slip, I slide. You pour, I hold the cup. You snore, I get no sleep. You itch, I scratch. I massage, you enjoy. I pet, you purr. I serva, you serve. I sell, you buy. I teach, you learn. You praise, I grow. I save, you inherit. You cook, I eat. You poop, I pamper. I spend, you earn. You advise, I benefit. You critique, I improve. You win, we both win. You tear, I repair. You break it, I fix it. I lose it, you find it. You lend, I repay. You mix it. I drink it. You mess it up, you clean it up. You talk, I listen. You sneeze, I gesundheit. You wish, I fulfill. You undress, I caress. You break, I mend. You design, I develop. You manufacture, I distribute. You call, I answer. I inflate it, you pop it. You sow, I reap. You prance, we dance. You offer, I accept. You regulate, I comply. You run, I chase. You send, I receive. You spill, I wipe. You snooze, you lose. You bake, I have cake. You create, I admire. You invite, I attend. You tax, I pay. You cast bread upon the water, you get soggy bread. You write, I read. You buy, I profit. You lick, I stick. You fly, I waive bye-bye. You celebrate, I reciprocate. You coordinate, I participate. You polish, I shine. You feed, I grow. You cry, I comfort. You hide, I seek. You drive, I ride. You fly, you get high. You anticipate, I appreciate. You smile, I smile, too. You hurt, I help. You ask, I tell. You supervise, I work. You manage, I produce. You promise, I accept. You lead, I follow. You dictate, I type. You request, I promise. You perform, I applaud. You joke, I laugh. You smoke, I cry. You stroll, I roll. You pray, God replies. You arrive, I welcome. You depart, I say goodbye. You propose, I agree. You trim, I look good. You consult, I am informed. You invoice, I pay. You peddle, I push. I write, you revise. You listen, you learn. You seek, you find. You cut, I polish. You perform, I am entertained. You slip, I slide. You pour, I hold the cup. You snore, I get no sleep. You itch, I scratch. I massage, you enjoy. I pet, you purr. I serve, you serve. We provide service to each other all our lives. Now, let's work together to *"UP Your Service!"*

What would *you* do?

A new competitor appears. Their advertising and promotions promise 'a new world of spectacular service'. You check carefully and discover their service level is no better than your own. And you've been delivering quality service for years. *What would you say to your customers?*

A customer is delighted with your service. She has written a letter of compliment and wants to know what else she can do to express apprecation to your staff. *What would you suggest?*

A new employee joins your organization. After a few weeks he starts to question why you work so hard to ensure such high levels of customer satisfaction. He wonders if your customers are really so particular. After all, they have been with you for years and seem unlikely to switch. *What would you say to him? What else would you do?*

One of your suppliers proposes a new joint venture. The logic of combining your resources is very good, but your service levels are quite different. *How would you proceed to give the new company the best chance for success?*

One of your long-serving staff has been cutting back on her efforts. Her service to customers and partners is declining. *How would you handle this situation?*

Your colleague comes to work in a bad mood. It is affecting his performance, and yours. *What would you say to him? What would you do?*

"The success of the enterprise is in your capable hands."

UP Your Service! action steps

Run a contest. Challenge your staff to explain, in 100 words or less, why providing great service to customers and colleagues makes good sense. Post or publish the entries where all staff can read them. Vote for the top three statements and award prizes to the winners.

Invite several of your best customers to a staff meeting. Ask them to describe what they appreciate most about your service. Give your staff and customers an opportunity to ask questions of each other.

Choose four or five complaint letters you have received in the past year. Read them out loud at a staff meeting. (Carefully remove specific names to avoid unnecessary embarrassment or humiliation.) Ask small groups to discuss each complaint and decide what would happen if you did nothing to improve or change in that area. Have each group make a brief presentation of their conclusions, and their suggestions for future action.

Review pages 8 and 9 in this chapter. What percentage of your customer base would you put in each of the categories shown? Have these percentages been changing over time? In which direction?

Visit three companies known for high levels of service. Interview several of the staff. Why are they so enthusiastic? What are they doing that works? What good ideas could you adopt or adapt? Is your team as committed? What seems to make the difference? *What have you learned from this exercise? Who can you share this with?*

"Step UP!"

2

It Takes an *UP Your Service!* Mindset

*Getting your service UP and keeping it UP
requires a major commitment.*

*It takes focus, time, ongoing effort
and continuous education.*

And, it can be done.

*All over the world,
people are taking practical steps
to understand their customers,
create positive impressions,
generate more service value,
develop long-term partnerships
and deepen loyalty for the future.*

You can do it, too.

*It begins with the people
who are on your team.*

*It all begins with an
UP Your Service!* **mindset**.

It takes an *UP Your Service!* mindset

UP Your Service! requires a special way of thinking, feeling and acting towards your customers. It's a state of mind, an attitude and a way of seeing the world that motivates you to give your very best. I call it an *UP Your Service!* **mindset**.

Six characteristics illustrate the *UP Your Service!* mindset. Which describe your company, your department and you?

1. Abundant generosity

Do you have a genuine desire to *give* to others? Do you like to hear people say, *"I got more than I expected!"*

Abundant generosity is how you make it happen.

You can be generous with your *time and expertise* by:

"It all begins up here!"

- showing someone how to use your service, install your system or better maintain your products,

- being exceptionally patient with a customer who is slow, frustrated or confused,

- staying 'after hours' to help, although it's officially time for your lunch, coffee-break or heading home for the day,

- assisting your colleague on a special project, even though it's not your job.

You can be generous with your *prices and products* by:

- giving a deal or a discount to a valued customer,

- recommending an inexpensive upgrade path to maximize their existing investments,

- extending a guarantee or special offer to increase the value of their purchase.

You can be generous with your *mood and manners* by:

- complimenting a customer on her purchase,

- thanking a colleague for his assistance,

- giving new staff an encouraging pat on the back,

- offering someone a business-building referral or a proactive piece of advice.

The Body Shop practices generosity with free giftwrapping, even for the smallest items purchased. **The Baker's Dozen** in London is a legend for giving more than 12 – you always get 13! **Comfort Taxi** in Singapore recognizes generous and honest behavior each month by publishing the names of drivers who return wallets and items left behind by passengers.

Generosity is not a natural way of thinking for some folks, and that's OK. If you are more keen to 'follow the rules' than 'follow your heart', you may be better off on the production line than on the front line. You choose!

*"THE MORE YOU GIVE, THE MORE YOU WILL RECEIVE.
LIFE IS A REPLENISHING RESOURCE."*

How abundantly generous are you?		
The less I give, the more I get to keep!	I give people exactly what they purchased. No more, no less.	I give others all I can. I like to go the 'extra mile'.
1 2	.... 3	4 5

2. Genuine compassion

When a person is complaining loudly, do you hear someone who really needs your help? When a customer is nasty and rude, do you offer calm and understanding? When you are tempted to react with sarcasm or anger, does your *compassion* prompt you to take another view?

To the angry customer do you say gently, *"You must be having a tough day. Let me see how I can help"*? To the befuddled sales clerk do you offer, *"Thanks for your assistance. I know this can be confusing"*? To the forever unsatisfied do you carefully state, *"It's OK. You deserve to get what you really want"*?

Compassionate folks know that customers and colleagues are basically good people (although they may suffer through occasional bad moments).

They might be frustrated by a personal difficulty, financial problem, family matter or a challenge with their health. You may never know the inside story, and it doesn't really matter.

Whether face-to-face, on the telephone, or sending out a message, your genuine compassion touches others with care and kind attention.

Globe Silk Store projects a caring, family image with special attention for mothers and children, a family-style cafeteria for customers and exceptional service quality training for all staff.

"LIFE IS NOT A ZERO SUM GAME. THE KINDNESS YOU SHOW OTHERS IS QUICKLY MULTIPLIED. MEANNESS IS DIVIDED."

How genuinely compassionate are you?		
Life is tough for everyone. Deal with it.	When others are nice to me, I return the favor.	I like to help people feel good. It makes me feel good, too.
1 .... 2 .... 3 .... 4 5		

3. The *'can-do'* spirit!

Do you have a positive outlook on your work and in your life? Or are you a gloomy cynic, a wet blanket, a cold shower on the enthusiasm of others?

Do you approach difficulties with enthusiasm, challenges with interest and commitment? Do you see problems as obstacles stuck in your way, or as opportunities in clever disguise?

Do you welcome complaints from customers as useful contributions? Do you appreciate gripes and groans from colleagues? Are these hassles to be avoided, or energy-loaded inputs to help you make things better?

Can you be trusted to keep your word, fulfill your promises and meet your obligations? Do you make the effort, go the extra mile, always keep in touch? Do you like to go *beyond the call of duty*, or do you settle for second best?

Andersen Consulting has built a worldwide reputation for reliable, on-time delivery. Their motto in the business world: *"We do whatever it takes."*

Are you the person others turn to for an upbeat point of view? Do you have, live, work and share a vibrant *'can-do'* spirit?

Nike embraces this commitment to achieve with their global advertising slogan. You know what it says, and what it means: *"Just do it."*

> *"CHALLENGE? I LOVE A CHALLENGE.*
> *WHAT WOULD LIFE BE WITHOUT A CHALLENGE?"*

Do you have the *'can-do'* spirit?		
Save your effort. Give up early. Life is pessimistic.	You get the good with the bad. Life is realistic.	I turn lemons into sweet lemonade. Life is optimistic!
1 .... 2 .... 3 .... 4 5		

4. Eagerness to learn and grow

Do you have an insatiable appetite to improve as a person, a colleague and an *UP Your Service!* provider?

Do you want to know more about every angle and aspect of your business? Who are your customers? How do they use your services and products? What do they value most? What new features has your company introduced? What are the benefits for your customers? Who are your top suppliers? What can they teach you now? Who are your best competitors? What are they doing differently and better than you?

Do you take every opportunity to upgrade your professional knowledge through conferences, seminars and workshops, presentations, publications, discussion groups, interactive message boards and industry-specific websites?

Do you have mentors who can help you grow and coaches who can train you? Do you have learning partners throughout the industry with whom you share ideas and exchange information?

At **Jollibee Restaurants** in the Philippines, learning is exalted as a fine art. Training is an ongoing passion. Annual events are veritable celebrations of education, motivation and new ideas.

Ken Blanchard, author of *The One Minute Manager*, says candid input from others is a key to your success. *"Feedback is the breakfast of champions."* Are you eager for input from your fan club *and* your critics? Are you getting a well-balanced breakfast of input and suggestions every day?

"Every waking moment is an opportunity to learn something new. Life offers an unlimited and ongoing education."

How eager are you to learn, improve and grow?		
Leave me alone. I have enough to do without you bothering me.	If the company pays for me to attend a seminar, I'll go.	I am eager for continuous improvement. What else can I do to grow?
1 2	 3	.... 4 5

5. Take personal responsibility

Are you the one who always asks, *"What can I do to make an improvement? How can this situation be made better?"*

Whatever the source or the cause for concern, do you waste time and energy laying blame, feeling shame and finding justifications? Or do you look for the clearest pathway forward: *"What action can I take right now?"*

If you make a mistake do you look for an excuse, or for what you can do to fix it?

When a customer approaches you with a question or problem, do you *own it* until it is resolved? If you pass it along to a colleague for help, or another department for resolution, do *you* make sure the correction is done? Do *you* confirm the customer is contented?

When the market changes and a competitor surges ahead, are you the one to notice? Do you count on Marketing to react in time, or do you send in suggestions, make recommendations and ensure the voice of your customer is heard?

If something breaks, do you wait for Engineering to discover and repair the flaw? Or are you the person who makes the call, writes it down and sends in the maintenance request?

Personal responsibility doesn't mean always knowing the answers. Sometimes the responsible thing to do is admit you are in over your head! At **FMC**, this is embedded in the culture with this phrase: *"A cry for help is a sign of strength."* Through direct action or conversation, make it happen now.

"IF IT'S GOING TO BE, IT'S UP TO ME."

Are you personally responsible?		
It's not my job. It's not my fault.	Who messed this up? Whose job is this anyway?	What can I do right now to make this better?
1 .... 2 .... 3 .... 4 5		

6. See the world from your customer's point of view

Do you realize the world you see is not the world your customers see? Customers have different concerns, preferences, backgrounds, needs, priorities and intentions.

When you wake up in the morning, who's looking out your eyes? It's you. When the phone rings, whose point of view do you answer from? Yours.

An e-mail comes from the boss. Whose point of view do you read it from? Yours. You attend the weekly department meeting. Whose point of view do you listen and participate from? Once again, it's yours.

Now go face-to-face with a customer. And whose point of view pops to mind? Surprise, surprise, *it's yours!*

It takes an *effort* to see the world from another person's point of view. *Do you actively make that effort?* Do you put yourself in the other's shoes, see the world from *their* perspective? Do you work hard to understand what others want and need right now?

At Heathrow Airport, **British Airways** took the bold step of installing a 'video feedback booth' for passengers to document their pleasures (compliments) and their pain (complaints). This powerful recording was shown to executives and managers at the highest levels of the organization. Face-to-face, they *saw the world* from their customers' point of view.

> "*EACH OF US SEES A DIFFERENT WORLD. IMAGINE WHAT VARIETY EXISTS THROUGH THE EYES OF THOSE AROUND YOU.*"

Do you see the world from your customers' point of view?		
The world is the way I see it. What I see is what you get.	I can see another point of view, but you have to show it to me clearly.	I make a real effort to see the world from others' viewpoints.
1 .... 2 .... 3 .... 4 5		

We become what we think about

Thought is creative and you are the thinker.

Fill your mind with angry thoughts and a mean world will surround you. Become a fountain of constructive thinking and an empire of good tidings will emerge.

Approach your world of service with caring, commitment and compassion. You will be richly rewarded with a joyful life and a successful, growing business.

"Those who bring sunshine into the lives of others, cannot keep it from themselves."
SIR JAMES M. BARRIE, AUTHOR OF 'PETER PAN'

What's your total score for an *UP Your Service!* mindset?

Your score	Ron's recommendation
1 - 9	Work with products, paper and procedures...not people!
10 - 18	Are you sure you really want to serve? You'll have to make some changes.
19 - 27	You have *UP Your Service!* potential. Keep on growing and giving.
28 - 30	You've got what it takes! Now, teach what you know to others!

What would *you* do?

A customer comes in with a complaint. Your staff member goes overboard trying to set things right, and gives away more than twice the value of the original order. He says you told him to be generous. *What would you do with this staff member? How would you use this experience to educate the entire organization?*

You have two staff eligible for promotion. One is extremely caring and concerned about staff welfare. The other is known for tackling tough issues head-on, getting things done in record time. There is only one staff position to be filled. *Which person would you choose? What would you say to the other?*

You hire a trainer to conduct a teambuilding program. One of your staff does not show up for the training. The next day she explains she was helping a customer resolve an important issue. *How would you respond? What actions would you take to follow up?*

To help a customer, one of your staff uses his personal access key to enter the building after hours. The customer is delighted by the special treatment, but the employee accidentally sets off an alarm that triggers an emergency police response. *How would you react in this situation? What would you say to the staff, to the customer, to the police?*

The economy is in a downturn. Your company needs better cash flow, but your customers need longer credit terms. *How do you resolve this apparent contradiction? What can you do for your customers? What can you do for the company?*

> *"Sometimes the questions are not easy.*
> *What decisions to make?*
> *Which actions to take?*
> *Ultimately, it's your choice."*

UP Your Service! action steps

Select the most service-oriented members of your team. Have them create a *code of service conduct* for the entire organization. Get feedback from others, fine-tune the wording, then publish and promote it widely.

Create a training program based upon your new code of service conduct. Highlight behaviors and examples that exemplify the code and those that violate its meaning. Use case studies and role plays to make the training realistic.

Become a customer of your own company, or another much like yours. Discover what it's like to be on the other side of the counter, the other end of the phone, the receiving side of your service. Rotate this assignment throughout your team. Then compare notes and generate ideas for improvement.

Practice generosity. Give away small gifts, unrequested extras, tokens of appreciation to your customers and your colleagues. Record what others say to you, and how you feel about it.

Set up an internal awards program. Recognize staff who go out of their way to help others. Create a *Wall of Fame* for those nominated and selected by their customers and peers.

Boost morale with 'quick wins'. Build towards high goals with many small successes. Celebrate each stage completely.

Monitor your own mindset.
When you are service focused, *serve!* When you are frustrated, *take a break!*

"Next step!"

3

It Takes an *UP Your Service!* Toolset

*Positive attitudes and good intentions are important,
but not enough to UP Your Service!*

*You also need proven tools, practical skills
and reliable, effective techniques.*

*Imagine trying to cultivate a garden
with lots of commitment but no
wheelbarrow, rakes or shovels.
What would you get?
Weeds.*

*Try building a house with wood and a plan,
but no hammers, ladders or saws.
What would you have?
Lumber.*

*If you want to serve customers
with grace and flair and
have clients who sing your praises,
you need more than just people with good ideas.*

*You need to create, upgrade and forever maintain
an UP Your Service!* **toolset.**

It takes an *UP Your Service!* toolset

You need the right gear to climb a mountain safely. You need excellent equipment to dive beneath the sea. To scale the heights of customer delight and recover from the depths of problems, you need tools and technology you can trust. You need an *UP Your Service!* **toolset** with these eight essential items.

1. Excellent products and services

Are your products and services amongst the finest available anywhere? In a worldwide search for best-in-class, will your offerings come out on top?

Is your company up-to-date with the latest innovations and improvements? Are you up-to-speed with the pace of change and new technologies in your field?

Are you constantly seeking to improve the products you sell? Are you fine-tuning every day to increase customer value?

Are your services innovative, cost-effective, reliable and unique? Do you modify, customize and tailor your offer to meet your customer's needs?

Your market is growing every day, and customers are spoiled for choice. **Sony** has built a loyal following by introducing new products every year. Are yours as fresh and creative?

"To win in today's competitive markets, you need to get volume (be the biggest) or get niche (be the best) or get out."

How good are your products and services?		
Barely good enough to keep us in the game.	We define the average. We are in the middle of the market.	We provide premium products and services.
1 .... 2 .... 3 .... 4 5		

2. Efficient delivery systems

Are your systems for product and service delivery accurate, fast and convenient? Is it easy for customers to place new orders and track existing orders with your user-friendly system?

Can your staff quickly locate important details about inventory levels, recent shipments, past billings and orders now in progress?

Do your customers have a choice of how and when to place their orders: over the counter or over the telephone, by fax, e-mail or quickly and easily at your website?

Can your customers choose when and how to take delivery: at home or at the office, in the evening or on the weekend? By courier, postal service or personal collection? In hard copy, on diskette, or by downloading directly from the Internet?

The world is getting faster and more connected every day. From smoke signals to digital signal processing. From dialing the operator to surfing the Web. From telegraphs to telephones to handheld cellular personal digital assistants.

Domino's Pizza created a whole new world with fast pizza delivery: *"In 30 minutes, pizza hot at your door, or it's free!"* Many companies offer the same today, but Domino's is the one remembered.

What about you? Are you ready and willing to serve your customers, when they want it, the way they want it, 24 hours a day, 7 days a week, 365 days a year?

If you are, keep doing it. If you're not, make it happen!

"I WANT IT FAST. I WANT IT HERE. I WANT IT NOW!"

How easy and efficient are your delivery systems?		
If you really want it, come pick it up during normal office hours.	Please be patient. We'll get it to you in a little while.	You can place an order, track an order or arrange delivery at any time.
1 2	.... 3 4	 5

3. Competent, well-trained people

Do all your team members know *what to do* and *how to do it well*? Are they recognized for their obvious skills and the quality of their service decisions?

Are your people consistently trained by the best professionals and programs in the business? Do you keep their skillset razor sharp? Is their motivation riding high?

Do your frontline staff have excellent listening skills, superior product knowledge and well-developed talent in interpersonal communications? Are they supported by a back-office team equally committed to *UP Your Service?*

Do your service providers apply best practices in telephone contact, consultative selling, complaint resolution and service recovery techniques? Do they have enough authority to give generously, recover quickly and bend the rules when needed?

Do your managers anticipate emerging employee and customer needs? Do they have the skills they need in coaching, counseling, leadership and supervision?

McDonald's is known throughout the world for Big Macs, french fries and the friendly Ronald McDonald. But it is also known, trusted and frequently praised for the consistent training of its people.

> *"IN A SERVICE BUSINESS (AND TODAY, ALL BUSINESSES ARE SERVICE BUSINESSES) THE FINAL FACTOR FOR SUCCESS AND GROWTH IS WELL-TRAINED, ENTHUSIASTIC PEOPLE."*

How competent and well-trained are your staff?		
Hey, we've got warm bodies. That's already an achievement!	We can handle the basics. Special requests take longer.	Our team is highly skilled and well-equipped. We have what it takes to delight you.
1 2	.... 3	4 5

4. User-friendly policies and procedures

UP Your Service! organizations are *easy to do business with.* Their policies and procedures are fast, convenient and user-friendly.

When prospects, customers and suppliers reach out to contact you, is the process for them smooth and easy?

Are they asked to provide essential information *just once?* Do they get a 'single point of contact' for all their questions, orders and communications? Or are they forced to navigate through layers of offices, departments and divisions?

In my family, we have two mobile phones, three incoming telephone lines, a fax line, a high speed line for video-conferencing and two Internet accounts. All are with the same telephone company. But each account requires a separate call to a different department if I have a question about the service. The only thing the telephone company has consolidated is the billing!

"You need the right tools for the job!"

This sends the customer the *wrong* message: *"We will make collecting your money very easy, but for you to get good service, it's hard!"*

When placing an order, can your customers mix and match, pick and choose and customize a selection to their liking?

Burger King has built a reputation for user-friendly policies and flexible orders from the menu. Their playful advertising sings the message clearly: *"Have it your way! Have it your way!"*

What is your policy for exchanges and returns? If someone wants to bring an item back, do you say, *"Fill out the form and talk to the manager"*, or do you welcome the exchange without a problem?

Giordano and **Land's End** have built tremendous goodwill by allowing customers to return products anytime.

Does your operating manual rigidly protect the company from the occasional scoundrel or cheat? Or do your policies trumpet loud and clear: *"We trust our customers! We value your business. We make it easy for you to get what you want."*

Your internal processes should be quick and easy, too. Think about these common procedures: purchase orders, equipment rental, maintenance requests, transfer forms, employee benefit programs, vacation requests and training program registration. Are these systems a pain in the neck or a pleasure for you to use?

Many company policies have long and strange histories, bureaucratic origins that may or may *not* be relevant today. Remember, great internal and external systems will boost productivity, passion and profits. How up-to-date and user-friendly are yours?

And finally, when routine systems just won't work, must you jump through hoops and walk across fire to make anything special happen? Or can you make a decision and bend the rules without your boss getting bent out of shape?

> *"MAKE IT SO EASY TO DO BUSINESS WITH YOU THAT IT'S NOT WORTH YOUR CUSTOMER'S TIME TO DO BUSINESS WITH ANYONE ELSE!"*

Are your policies and procedures 'user-friendly'?		
Customers cannot be trusted. Our policies are designed to protect us.	Things have always been this way. Why change now?	We fine-tune our systems constantly. Customer convenience is our mission.
1 2	.... 3	4 5

5. Customer information database

Do you have a comprehensive mechanism for learning about your customers and sharing information over time? Do you know where your customers come from, what they really want, when, how and where they like to order? Do you know what they purchase, how they use it and their current level of customer satisfaction?

Do you know when they are likely to need more of your product or service? Are you sure about how they prefer to be contacted, and contracted, in the future?

Does your system identify customers with high lifetime value for special care and consideration? Does it point out which customers are most likely to change providers for more immediate and generous attention?

Is a complete record of all customer contact easily available to everyone in the company who sees and serves your customer?

Is information from each new contact automatically collected, quickly organized and displayed in an integrated and user-friendly system?

Can your customers enter this database themselves to update, correct or add new information to help you serve them better?

American Express has built a legendary system for knowing, tracking and assisting customers worldwide. Wherever you are, whatever you need, they have the tools to help you.

"THE MORE YOU KNOW ABOUT YOUR CUSTOMERS,
THE BETTER YOU CAN SERVE THEM NOW AND THE MORE
LIKELY YOU ARE TO KEEP THEM IN THE FUTURE."

How complete is your customer information database?		
Have you ever bought anything from us before?	I've got your information around here somewhere. Can you hold a few minutes?	Your complete customer history is with me now. How can I help you?
1 2	 3	.... 4 5

6. Comprehensive feedback systems

Are your customers regularly surveyed for their impressions, preferences and suggestions? Is this valuable information used proactively to create new products and services?

Whether customers are browsing, shopping, selecting, buying, paying, receiving, using, misusing, returning, questioning, praising or complaining, do you have open channels to actively solicit and receive their feedback?

Do you have suggestion boxes, telephone hotlines, live interviewers, comment cards, questionnaires, evaluation forms, e-mail addresses, website pages and video feedback booths strategically placed as *listening posts* to capture customers' ideas, complaints and suggestions?

When your customers *do* reply, do you respond to them right away? Are their efforts to communicate genuinely praised? Is their initiative quickly rewarded?

Finally, do you have a system for keeping track of all these complaints, compliments and suggestions? You need to watch the trends over time to know which way you're headed!

At **Four Seasons Hotels** around the world, every guest is queried politely to ensure they are completely satisfied with their stay and with the service. Throughout the hotel, at reservations, room service, laundry, dining, poolside, bedside and in the restaurants, the friendly and dedicated staff want your answer to this key question: *"Are you completely satisfied? If we could do one thing to make your visit even better, what would it be?"*

How effective is your feedback system?		
Don't call us. We'll call you. 'Customer comments' are a pain in the neck.	We fix things when customers complain. The squeaky wheel gets the grease.	We seek out candid feedback and respond quickly to customers' suggestions.
1 2	 3	.... 4 5

7. A system for continuous improvement

Do you have a company-wide system for continuous improvement, including active suggestion schemes, cross-functional quality teams, work improvement contests and benchmarking programs inside and outside the industry?

Do you use proven quality improvement techniques such as key result areas and key service indicators, root cause analysis, work flow process mapping and statistical evaluation? Do you set and maintain high standards, pacing yourself against world class criteria of industry certification and annual competitive ranking? Are you as tough on yourself as your customers are on you?

Do you seek public recognition and internal motivation by competing against the best for a full range of national and international awards?

In the personal computer industry, the people who make *Quicken* software, **Intuit**, have an award-winning reputation leading to confidence and loyalty from customers.

Other software programs have equivalent price and features, but no one has Intuit's reputation for customer sensitivity and ongoing improvement in documentation, website, free e-mail updates, call-center excellence and 24-hour technical support.

Motorola runs a *Total Customer Satisfaction* contest each year to reduce defects, improve speed, minimize waste, maximize profits and ramp up customer delight.

> *"GOOD, BETTER, BEST? NEVER LET IT REST, UNTIL YOUR GOOD IS BETTER AND YOUR BETTER IS THE BEST."*

Do you have a system for continuous improvement?		
When it breaks, we figure out a way to fix it.	If it isn't broken, don't mess with it. Why make trouble?	We work to make things better *right now*, long before they break.
1 .... 2 .... 3 .... 4 5		

8. Effective organizational structure

The right organizational structure facilitates collection of talent, sharing of views, rapid decisions, flexible execution and quick responses to unexpected opportunities or problems.

'Chain of command' may be good for a marching army, but it has real limitations for creating new service value in a dynamic global market. Customer expectations can change in a minute. How fast can your company respond?

At **Cap Gemini Ernst & Young**, project teams come together and disband when each assignment is done. **Citibank** is constantly flexing between centralized and decentralized models. They don't consider one approach *better* than the other. Instead, they look for new ways to generate value every time they change!

Some organizations change positions frequently as a way of developing staff and bringing up fresh ideas. The **Government of Singapore** employs this approach with vigor, moving key players into and out of industry, regulatory, administrative and executive positions.

You can organize around product lines, technologies or the processes in your business. You can take a geographic view, arranging your team by country, language, custom or religion. You can even let personal preferences and talents rule the day.

Whatever your current structure or approach, keep this fact in mind: the measure of your success is the level of service you provide and the total satisfaction of your customers.

"Change is good."

How effective is your organizational structure?		
Our structure was created in the era of pyramids and the Sphinx. We are bureaucratic.	We avoid reorganization except when absolutely necessary to survive. We are pragmatic.	We reorganize quickly to suit the customer and the market. We are dynamic.
1 2	 3	.... 4 5

Keep your toolset up-to-date!

Many years ago, tools were the key to your profession. The builder, blacksmith, cobbler, farmer, seamstress, physician and cabinet-maker all depended upon their tools for their livelihoods and their success. Apprentices learned from journeymen who learned in turn from masters of the trade.

Today, tools are evolving quickly. New technologies emerge overnight, transforming the business and service landscape: software, hardware, insights and new approaches, paradigms, programs, and endless possibilities to innovate and grow.

There is no longer a single 'master' who can teach all you need to know. You must keep your interest keen, your appetite to learn forever hungry.

Become an expert where you can. But always be ready to start again, to become, when needed, a beginner.

"ONLY A LIFE LIVED IN SERVICE TO OTHERS IS WORTH LIVING."
ALBERT EINSTEIN

What's your total score for an *UP Your Service!* toolset?

Your score	Ron's recommendation
1 - 10	No system. No tools. No structure. Pretty soon, no customers!
11 - 20	You are vulnerable and can be pushed aside quickly by decent competition.
21 - 30	You have laid a good foundation. Keep moving and improving.
31 - 40	You are strong and growing stronger day by day. You can lead the field!

What would *you* do?

You plan to improve efficiency by centralizing customer service on the World Wide Web. But your customers are accustomed to getting personalized service over the telephone and at your outlets. *How would you plan this transformation? What would you tell your customers and when?*

You have a budget to improve staff welfare. You can use it for additional training, more telephone lines or to purchase some new computers. *Which would you choose? How would you decide?*

Bureaucracy is a nightmare in your organization. It's slowing the company down, stifling innovation and upsetting your customers. You have been asked to propose two entirely new structures for management review. *Where would you begin? Who would you ask to work with you on this project?*

You implement a new feedback system and complaints come pouring in. More compliments come in, too. The workload in replying is substantial. Some say it would have been better to leave things as they were. *What do you think? What would you do?*

You win industry awards for quality of product, speed of delivery and operational excellence. But your market share is declining. Your customers are defecting to other service providers. *What could be going wrong? Why might this be happening? What should you and your colleagues do about it?*

"Not sure what to do? Keep calm and keep thinking. Good answers are right up here!"

UP Your Service! action steps

Identify two training programs you or your staff will need in the near future. Surf the World Wide Web for companies and courseware that will meet this emerging need.

Send a letter of complaint, compliment or suggestion to six different companies, each in a different industry. Keep track of the replies you receive. Which replies boost your sense of loyalty to the company? Which seem rigid or bureaucratic?

Analyze the organizational structure of other companies in your industry. How does their structure differ from your own? What are the advantages or disadvantages of each? Share your findings and lead a discussion amongst your colleagues and the management team.

Repeat the same process with leading companies *outside* your industry. What can you learn from this exercise? What can you change or apply in your own organization?

Make a list of things your customers ask for that your policies or procedures do not allow. What would need to change in order to accommodate these customer requests? Should you make the changes? Why, or why not?

Design the ideal customer information database. Write down everything you want to know and understand about your customers. How can you get all the information and make it available to the right people on your team? What first step can you take, right now?

"One more step!"

4

It Takes an *UP Your Service!* Culture

*What makes a nation great, an army strong,
a restaurant noted for its service?*

*What makes a community healthy, a school
successful? What will make your company succeed?*

*It's not just the people. It's not just the tools.
It's the **culture** that reinforces both.*

*Culture is the glue that binds
people and systems together.
It's the context that shapes the expectations of
your customers and the performance of your staff.*

*You've hired and promoted people
with a winning service **mindset**.
(Use Chapter 2)*

*You've created and fine-tuned
a terrific service **toolset**.
(Apply Chapter 3)*

*Now let's build an UP Your Service! **culture**
to keep your mindset growing and
your toolset razor sharp.*

It takes an *Up Your Service!* culture, too!

Culture sets the standards. It lets people know what's accepted, rewarded and forbidden. It is the context that surrounds your staff, supports their actions and keeps them focused on the goal. Culture is the modus operandi of your team, it's *"the way we get things done"*.

Your culture can be loose or tight, open or restricted. It can be spontaneous or highly structured, traditional, innovative, predictable, performance-oriented or even 'off the wall'.

Culture can be customer-focused or product-centric, cost-controlling or revenue-driven. It can be exciting and challenging or downright depressing and destructive.

Culture can be crafted, shaped and created intentionally. It can also drift and decay without your careful attention.

Here are 15 proven ways you can build an *UP Your Service!* culture that serves, sizzles and succeeds.

1. Your service philosophy

Are your service vision, mission and core values clearly articulated and written down in black and white? Have they been printed, framed and hung upon the wall? If so, that's a good start.

But where are they now?

All too often these important statements become part of the woodwork, ignored by old-timers and quickly forgotten by new hires. Don't let this happen to you.

Integrate key statements of your purpose and service philosophy into your performance management system: recruitment and orientation programs, training and development schemes, internal company communications, appraisal, recognition and rewards.

Ask yourself this question: *"Can every member of your staff explain the organization's service beliefs and values in their own words, and give practical illustrations from the course of their daily work?"* If so, you are harnessing the power of alignment and understanding. If not, your team may be adrift without a clear course, or rowing hard, but in divergent or conflicting directions.

Your service vision should not be fixed in stone. It must mature as you grow. At **Prudential Assurance** in Singapore, the company spent years bringing this mission statement to life:

"To be the best life insurer, exceeding our customers' expectations with quality people, excellent products and legendary service."

With focused effort, the statement rang true. Now the company is revising it towards a new threshold of ambition and intention:

"To be Asia's Number One in providing financial solutions,
#1 in customer focus,
#1 in creating shareholder value, and
#1 in attracting the best people."

Both declarations have been backed up by carefully crafted core values, management communications, company contests and countless hours of training to build internal alignment.

Build *your* service philosophy statement to be one of the best. Do the exercise in Chapter 11, *Craft Your Service Vision.*

"WITHOUT VISION, THE PEOPLE PERISH."
THE BIBLE

Are your service vision and philosophy crystal clear?		
We sell products and make profits. Who cares about customers?	We have a mission statement but no one ever reads it. Who wrote it anyway?	We embrace our service philosophy. Now watch us make it come alive!
1 2	.... 3 4	 5

2. New staff recruitment

Selecting great staff is the first step in building your team. How do you make sure every new hire agrees with your service vision and is aligned with your service values?

Do you give new staff candidates time to get to know you, your customers and your organization *before* they sign the contract? Do you use insightful interview techniques and profiling tools to ensure a good match between person and position?

Or do you complain about the tight labor market and try to hire enough warm bodies? If so, you may not understand the cost, in money and morale, of the resignations that will surely follow. It's time for you to take a new accounting.

Southwest Airlines involves current staff and loyal customers in their new employee selection process. They look for eager smiles and extra miles. And they turn down applicants who don't measure up.

The people they finally choose deliver a special brand of *Positively Outrageous Service*. And they tend to stick around – loyal, committed and highly motivated – for years.

At **Novell,** staff are encouraged and rewarded for bringing friends and family members into the company. They are not afraid of close relatives working together – *they encourage it!*

Cisco Systems constantly trolls the Internet seeking new staff. You can visit their website and be connected to a real employee to ask real questions and get real answers, in real-time.

"Well begun is half done."

How do you select and hire new staff?		
Are you breathing? Can you type? OK, you've got the job.	Your resume looks OK. Let's get you started now and see how it goes.	You chose us. We have carefully chosen you. Welcome aboard!
1 2	.... 3 4	 5

3. New staff orientation

A detailed study at **Texas Instruments** revealed this: employees who receive thorough and thoughtful orientation stay longer, serve better and contribute more to the team.

Is your current orientation program a boring review of the organization chart, vacation policy and dental benefits program? Are you investing enough to guarantee your new staff start out right?

A winning orientation program addresses seven vital issues:

- *Create comfort and rapport.* Make the first impressions count. Send company literature and a warm, personalized welcome letter to each new employee's home *before* they start to work. Your staff will feel great and their family members will appreciate it, too.

  "Build a company culture that turns your people ON!"

  Prepare a work space in advance. Get name-cards printed, new computers installed, and an e-mail address quickly established.

  Send a brief introduction of the new staff to all current members of your team. Post a new staff announcement on the bulletin board or broadcast it through your company-wide e-mail system.

  During the first few weeks, check in often. Call them up, take them to lunch, meet in the hallways and chat over coffee or tea. Do what it takes to make them feel good. Let them know they are welcomed and wanted.

- *Introduce the company culture.* Assign a 'buddy' to help new staff understand how things get done. Pick a peer-level and totally enthusiastic employee for this important role, someone who is committed to *UP Your Service!*

  Show new staff your *Hall of Fame* and explain how the awards are won. Let them know what's paramount to succeed and what kind of actions are encouraged.

  Provide a senior-management mentor for the first few years for career guidance and high level motivation.

- *Show the big picture.* How are you structured? Who is in charge? Where do people go to get things done?

  Who are your customers, what do they want, why do they come to you? What are their expectations, how are they changing and what are you doing to meet them?

  Who are your competitors? What are they doing right, what are they doing different? What are you doing to beat them?

  What are the trends, what's in the future, how is technology changing? Is the industry setting slowly, rising fast or in the midst of a complete transformation?

  At **Singapore Press Holdings**, a unique five-day management orientation program brings together new staff from editorial, marketing, production, distribution and support to learn together, and from each other, about the gestalt of the newspaper publishing business.

- *Explain job responsibilities.* Be clear with new staff about what is expected and how they will be appraised. Review and confirm all performance standards.

Set goals for personal achievement, then lock in dates to review the goals and objectives together.

- *Give and get feedback.* Dialog builds commitment. Make orientation a two-way street. Use panel discussions, question and answer sessions, and informal 'chats' with the bosses.

New employees can bring a valuable new perspective. Gain their input, seek their ideas and cover a wide range of issues.

- *Handle administrative matters.* Every new hire needs forms to be filled, but make it as pain-free as possible. Use on-line screens to collect the data. Make it user-friendly and easy to follow.

- *Provide a reality check.* Before new staff run off to work with visions of instant glory, tell them honestly about what can go wrong: the burnout, confusion and rejection.

Better that someone knows what to expect than to believe they have found Nirvana. Help staff anticipate what can go wrong and to whom they can turn for assistance.

Remember, orientation is not a job for Human Resources or the Personnel and Staffing Department. It's a crucial introduction for new members of your team. Everyone has a role to play. Get the whole company involved.

For an in-depth article on new staff orientation, read *It Pays to Help New Staff Start Right*. It's free at the website.

"GIVE ME A LEVER LONG ENOUGH AND A FIRM PLACE TO STAND, AND I CAN MOVE THE EARTH."
ARCHIMEDES

How do you help your new staff start right?		
Are you the new guy around here? The last one left last week.	That's your chair and your phone. Let me know if you have any questions.	Orientation lasts a few months. We'll do all we can to help you.
1 2	.... 3 4	 5

4. Training and development

Do you offer education and service development programs to help your people achieve their best?

Are you providing quality training in three key service areas?

- *Core service skills:* understanding customers, creating positive impressions, improving existing service, creating new service offers, generating value for customers, working with service partners inside and outside the company, resolving service problems and learning from service evaluation results.

- *Complementary service skills:* empathetic listening, interpersonal communication, teamwork, project management leadership, supervision, cultural awareness, motivation and emotional intelligence.

- *Industry-specific service skills:* product knowledge and process expertise, proficiency in your tools, technologies and procedures.

Are you employing a range of training techniques to fit the place, the people and the topics?

Use *role plays* to build those interpersonal skills that must be delivered live. Create study groups and cross-functional teams to build collaborative service solutions. Offer self-paced learning with tests and texts and easy-to-contact advisors.

Use websites and e-mail to keep learning fresh and up-to-date. **Hewlett Packard** uses on-line education to digitize – and popularize – staff training around the world.

Make sure that learning doesn't stop when the lessons for the day are done. Document and circulate interesting case studies as soon as they occur. Provide effective job aids to keep learning close to mind and key principles close at hand.

Gather feedback from participants and instructors to continually improve your courses. Conduct post-course evaluations to confirm business results and measure lasting value.

Motorola University pioneered assessment with four levels of educational review. You can use this too:

1. How much did you enjoy the course?
2. What did you learn that's useful?
3. How can you apply what you have learned?
4. Does the application of your learning produce new value for the business?

Are you squeezing value from every training dollar spent and every precious moment of your staff's attention? Do you assign study partners who stay in touch well beyond the classroom?

In customer service training at **OCBC Bank**, everyone writes down specific action steps to be taken over the next two weeks. Each person selects a buddy to call them two weeks later and check if the action step is complete. If it is, the buddy submits a brief completion report.

At the end of the month, the bank draws names and gives away hundreds of movie tickets to those who took the actions and the buddies who helped to follow up.

Remember, customer contact can be rewarding, but it can be difficult and demanding, too. Be sure your training boosts morale, builds the team and keeps motivation riding high.

"IF PEOPLE ARE YOUR GREATEST ASSET, THEN TRAINING IS A WISE FINANCIAL INVESTMENT."

How potent are your training and development programs?		
Who's not busy around here? Send them for some training.	More customer complaints? Better bring in another training program.	Our training is highly customized and fine-tuned for results!
1 2	 3	.... 4 5

5. Rewards and recognition

People thrive on praise and acclamation. Are your recognition programs both inspiring and effective?

Do you have contests to reinforce your service values? Do you give individual and team awards for achieving customer delight? Do you highlight letters of compliment with praise, prizes and promotions?

Recognition can be given in many ways and all of them can be effective. Use public events, private conversations, formal announcements, informal awards, planned ceremonies, unexpected gifts, elegant trophies, simple notes, prestigious plaques, colorful ribbons and one-of-a-kind celebrations.

At **World of Sports,** a brass bell hangs from the ceiling near the check-out counter. A sign invites customers to ring the bell if they have received impeccable service. When the bell is rung loudly, everyone wins: the whole team feels rewarded.

At **Singapore Airlines,** the Deputy Chairman's Award is the most prestigious tribute an employee can receive. The award is given each year to staff members or teams whose actions exemplify the airline's commitment to total quality service.

Winners are celebrated, photographed, interviewed, published, wined, dined and praised. But they receive no quick promotion nor monetary award. These people become role models, their stories retold by others as legends of service achievement. Recognition *is* the reward.

"WHAT GETS REWARDED — GETS DONE."

How does your company recognize and reward great service?		
You did a good job. But that IS your job. What do you want, a medal?	If a customer sings our praises loud, the company will take notice.	These awards are unique and effective. They help our staff stay motivated and service focused.
1 .... 2 .... 3 .... 4 5		

6. Appraisal and promotions

If you want an *UP Your Service!* team, have you made quality service (internal and external) a key component in your appraisals?

If you want creativity, do you recognize staff for their innovative contributions and reward them for new ideas?

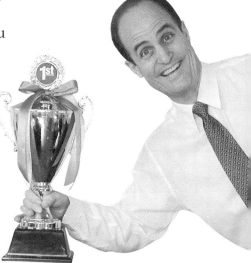

If you want to be led by champions who truly put the customer first, do you promote the staff who take a risk, or are they penalized for every error?

If you want an open corporate culture, are your appraisals in an open format?

"Link rewards and recognition with your appraisals and promotions to build a team of world-class winners!"

If you want a 'flat' organization, open communication and cross-functional exchange, do you employ 360-degree evaluations with candid feedback shared from above, alongside and below?

Take a close look at your current appraisal system. Does it help identify, reinforce and promote what you want your company to become? If it does, keep it. If not, change it.

"A GOOD COMPANY IS KNOWN BY THE PEOPLE IT KEEPS."

How do you evaluate, appraise and promote?		
Our annual appraisal is behind closed doors. It's a mystery to me.	Sometimes turkeys get promoted. I think seniority counts.	Our appraisal system works. The best people move ahead. Everyone understands why.
1 2	 3	.... 4 5

7. Company social events

Many company social events are lots of fun but lack business impact and value. Don't waste your money on a dinner and dance called *Disco Pirates of the '50s.*

You can provide enjoyment for your staff *and* generate strong enthusiasm for the company's goals and achievements.

Don't leave everything to an outside meeting planner for your next family day or other special function. Don't let the hotel staff, the catering team or the disco dynamos determine your program's tone and tenor.

Instead, pick a team of energetic new hires to conceive and create your next company social event. Choose a theme that links your people with your service improvement goals: *Reach for the Top, Gold-Plated Service, Delighting Our Customers Together.* Set a timeline and a budget, but let the innovation be their own.

Reward staff for providing the entertainment with skits, songs, dancing, mock advertisements, quiz shows and debates. Give prizes for commitment, creativity and connection to service values. Invite customers and suppliers as company guests, and as impartial judges for the scoring.

When it's over, lavish praise on all for a creative event well done. Replay the video in the staff cafeteria. Post copies of the photos on the wall. Build a tradition for celebration and social interaction that fortifies your culture as it grows.

"WE ENJOY IT MORE WHEN WE DO IT OURSELVES."

How does your company gather for social events?		
Our dinner and dance is so boring. Two speeches, one dance and we all leave after the last Lucky Draw.	Our social events are lots of fun. I'll bet they cost a bundle. Actually, I'd rather see it in my bonus.	Our events are a high-light of the year. We celebrate and motivate together. Inspiring!
1 2	 3	.... 4 5

8. Internal communications

Is it easy for your people to be in communication with one another right away? Are calls and pages returned promptly? Is voicemail answered quickly? Are faxes returned the very next day? Is e-mail answered within hours?

Do your staff use e-mail, voicemail, pagers, mobile telephones, company websites and FAQs to keep everyone in the loop? Do they use groupware, shared calendars, bulletin boards, automated movement displays and weekly meetings to keep their colleagues up-to-date?

What about your company memos? Are they dry, officious and boring? Is that the kind of place you want your organization to be? Are your bulletin boards covered with old announcements and faded pieces of tape? Or are they current, colorful and always a source of useful information?

Is your internal newsletter a respected forum, or is it sanitized propaganda from Head Office? Does it highlight complaints and compliments from real customers? Does it focus on difficult issues and challenging but significant achievements? Or is it full of pomp and too many pictures of the boss, which inspires and motivates no one.

The good news you will always get – it's the bad news that really counts. Service *problems* demand communication. How fast does your organization spread the word?

> *"IF YOU ARE NOT PART OF THE SOLUTION,*
> *YOU ARE PART OF THE PROBLEM."*

How fast and informative are your internal communications?		
If you want to know what's really going on, spend your time in the restrooms.	I can usually find out what's happening, but it takes a while. Information moves slowly around here.	Questions move quickly and answers are widely known. We thrive on candid communication.
1 2	 3	.... 4 5

9. Management and staff interaction

The more your people interact, the better they will understand each other, serve one another and produce high performance.

Do you create frequent opportunities for dialog between your shifts, departments and divisions? Do you foster open communication between all levels of management and staff?

Do you schedule cross-functional meetings, panel discussions, shared coffee-breaks and regular off-site events? Do you encourage questions and answers, wide-ranging debates and probing, insightful conversations? Do you give people every chance to share their viewpoints and know each other better?

Have you extended this approach to include your customers and suppliers? Do you involve them in your design meetings, focus groups, product planning and service satisfaction surveys? Have you sent your staff out to meet customers where they live? Have you met with suppliers on their home ground to see exactly where and how they work?

The more people think about, talk about and learn about each other, the better they will cooperate and collaborate on creating an *Up Your Service!* future.

At the **Massachusetts Institute of Technology**, brown bag lunches are a cherished ritual for faculty, administrators and students. All gather during lunchtime to listen and speak out on important topics of the day.

*"IF YOU WANT FAMILY, YOU'VE GOT
TO MIX PEOPLE TOGETHER."*

How frequent and fruitful is your interaction?		
We work in silos around here. I do my job, you do yours. Customers and vendors are outside altogether.	We can meet if you have a problem. But customers belong to Sales. Vendors go to Purchasing.	We mix and mingle often with colleagues, customers and vendors. It helps a lot to know each other well.
1 2	.... 3 4	 5

10. Physical atmosphere and ambience

Physical surroundings affect your customers and impact your team every day. Does your atmosphere help to *UP Your Service?*

For your customers: Have you built facilities to meet their needs, with decor to please their perceptions?

Are your floors, walls, ceiling, hallways, waiting areas and rest-rooms maintained in an attractive condition? Is your physical location lit well and kept at an appropriate temperature with a good circulation of fresh air? Do you manage the sounds around your space, or is the radio occasionally blaring?

Singapore's **Changi International Airport** spends millions on fresh orchids, tropical fish, new carpets, special lighting, inter-active kiosks, cactus gardens and even pre-recorded sounds of birds chirping in delight. Is it worth the cost and effort? They've been rated No. 1 in the world many times. How about you?

Your website is also a space where customers come to explore and conduct business. Is yours helpful, attractive, easy-to-navigate, comprehensive and fast-loading?

Porsche has built a global web presence as finely engineered as their legendary cars. In their showrooms and on the Web, customers feel the power and prestige of a Porsche.

For your staff: Do you provide a suitable blend of personal space and common areas, including work stations, meeting rooms, conference facilities, parking, pantry, library and a staff lounge for relaxation?

At the **SAS Institute**, a wooded campus setting is enhanced by on-site child-care, a health care center and sports facilities.

Do you have the appropriate tools, technology and equipment ready and close at hand? Are your computers plentiful and up-to-date, or grinding away in obsolescence?

Are motivational messages provided where they will be most encouraging and effective?

At the **National Eye Centre** in Singapore, customer compliments are posted in the lobby with photos of the staff and a certificate of appreciation from the Managing Director. What a great way to motivate employees and put customers in the right frame of mind!

At **United Artists Theaters**, mirrors at the counter remind ticket sales staff to make eye contact and share a welcoming smile.

Do you display information to keep your team in touch with customers and the realities of your business?

At **Intel**, manufacturing yields are posted in the staff cafeteria.

At **Manulife**, quarterly targets are listed in the office with names of the highest performing agents.

"Keep your business looking good. Little things do count!"

At **Philips**, photographs of real customers hang on the walls in call centers around the world.

What about your locations? Do they build staff pride and encourage interaction? Do they educate, motivate and inspire?

*"WHEN YOUR BUSINESS LOOKS GOOD, PEOPLE FEEL GOOD.
AND WHEN PEOPLE FEEL GOOD, THEY TREAT EACH OTHER WELL."*

How attractive is your organization's atmosphere and ambience?		
This place is truly ugly. No wonder the mood is, too.	The office is adequate to meet our needs. We are the industry average.	This work space really turns us on. And our customers love it, too!
1 2	 3	.... 4 5

11. Rites, rituals and traditions

Organizations with strong service cultures build enduring traditions to anchor their core values, celebrate service achievements and recall milestone events.

Ethnic and religious groups do this with special rites and ceremonies for holidays, weddings, funerals and births. Nations build commitment with flags and anthems, parades, pageants, pledges and oaths of allegiance.

Your company may not be as old as a nation or as potent as a worldwide religion, but you can use the same techniques to pull your people by their hearts and keep them bound together.

Do you have an emotional initiation ceremony to celebrate new hires when they join the company? At **SATS**, new hires must produce and perform service songs and skits to demonstrate their commitment to customers and to the company. Emotion runs high at these incredible events. The new staff are so proud. Existing staff members scream with applause. And members of the management team are inspired once again to keep promoting their *UP Your Service!* culture.

What's this crazy notion of throwing a party when someone decides to resign? The celebration should happen when people are hired or on their anniversary of joining the team!

Have you created a ritual of company pride to acknowledge long service, new products, customer compliments and sought-after staff promotions?

At **Microsoft**, new product launches are recorded forever in brass plaques embedded along the walkways.

In our office, a *Hall of Fame* showcases extraordinary staff and their legendary service achievements. A book of customer testimonials is kept close at hand to keep the team motivated and aligned towards our goals.

Do you have a service cheer, a pledge, a song, or another way for staff to reinforce and demonstrate their commitment?

At **Sony**, staff at all levels wear similar vests and exercise in the morning together. In the Japanese culture, this helps create a family of unity and strength and builds staff commitment.

Do your meetings start with commitment and end with a bang of enthusiasm, or a whimper of uncertainty and confusion?

At **Standard Chartered Bank**, management and customer service staff sign a common pledge each year to achieve their revenue and service targets.

At **IBM**, a top salesperson sounds a gong to start the monthly meeting. It's a position of honor and everyone applauds the service leader swinging the mallet.

How about you? What memorable means can you devise to build enthusiasm for your team, department or organization? What traditions can you begin or maintain to create positive emotions for customers and provide spectacular service?

This is not a facile, feel good exercise that's nice to have when other business issues are resolved. It's a critical issue to build commitment and gain the devotion of your people.

You can build your culture by thoughtful design or let it drift away by default.

"I PLEDGE ALLEGIANCE TO THE FLAG..."

How do you bond your team to higher levels of commitment?		
Our rituals are out of date. The excitement is gone. The fire went out years ago.	We drink beer together on Friday nights and buy lottery tickets at lunchtime.	Our traditions are alive with meaning and purpose. We celebrate our shared commitment!
1 2	 3	.... 4 5

12. Staff suggestion schemes

The staff suggestion program should be a vital element of your evolving company culture. But don't just hang boxes on the wall and wait for great ideas to come pouring in. They won't.

Instead, make your program come alive with a generous and innovative approach.

First, give prizes that people really want for great ideas submitted. Offer cash, dinner vouchers, movie tickets, fashionable products, training programs, gift certificates, magazine subscriptions, even time off from work. Find out what your staff truly enjoy and value. Then give it away in recognition of their best improvement ideas.

Second, change the criteria for winning on a regular or rotating basis: cost savings, income growth, incremental improvements, quantum shifts, quick-fixes, atmosphere enhancement, new staff recruitment and, ultimately, customer delight. You can even run a suggestion scheme for best ideas to improve the suggestion scheme!

Third, make your decisions quickly! No one wants to submit an idea and then wait six weeks for a cautious decision from The Committee.

At **Nissan Motors**, ideas are welcome from employees in writing, by telephone, on e-mail, through the corporate Intranet or in conversation face-to-face. They do whatever it takes to keep participation and enthusiasm growing.

"LET'S MAKE THIS PLACE EVEN BETTER. WHAT IS YOUR SUGGESTION?"

How vibrant is your staff suggestion scheme?		
We have a suggestion box on the wall. Mostly it's used to hold scrap paper.	Our 'ideas in action' program is pretty good, but it takes forever to get an answer.	We get a steady flow of great ideas. And we give out terrific prizes!
1 2	.... 3 4	 5

13. Community relations

How your organization interacts with the community at large impacts on the morale of your staff.

Do your people take pride in the advertising and public relations of your company? Are they proud to tell others where they work? Is your corporate image fresh and attractive, or stale, crusty and outdated?

Is your organization recognized as a public-spirited contributor to the health and welfare of the community? Or are you seen as just another money-making enterprise?

Asia Pacific Breweries sponsors sports and adventure events to boost their famous Tiger brand. And when grateful locals choose a favorite beer, it's always *"Give that man a Tiger!"*

APB also supports *Drink and Don't Drive* campaigns on television, in the press, on radio and at their website. They demonstrate commitment to their customers by connecting positively with the community at large.

What about your organization? Do you sponsor sports, promote the arts, encourage recycling, support youth activities, or contribute to renovation or historical reconstruction projects?

What kind of charities do you support? How many college internships do you provide? Are you involved with local schools, the elderly, minorities and differently-abled people?

> *"BUSINESS THRIVES IN HEALTHY COMMUNITIES.*
> *HELP YOUR COMMUNITY GROW."*

How well does your organization contribute to the community at large?		
Nothing special about us. We provide some jobs, but make no other contribution.	We react when community issues require a response. We stay out of the news and stick to our business.	We are proactive in providing assistance. We want to make this community even better.
1 2	.... 3 4	 5

14. Management role modeling

One of the most powerful ways to build company culture is for managers to lead by example. Talk with your customers. Spend time working on the frontline. Ask for, and listen to, staff suggestions. Respond quickly to all complaints. Be seen taking action to make things work out better.

The challenge for everyone who leads is clear: we must truly 'walk the talk'.

A senior executive from **Matsushita** was visiting one of the company's many manufacturing plants overseas. As he walked along the red carpet laid out on the factory floor, he saw a bit of paper below one of the large machines in the distance.

To his subordinates' shock and amazement, he detoured from the carefully prepared route and then stooped down to pick up the small scrap of paper. Placing it quietly into his pocket, he returned to the designated path.

Nothing more was said. But that one gesture did more to reinforce the company's commitment to housekeeping than countless booklets, banners and speeches. That one detour from the red carpet became a company legend, with a lesson.

Do your staff hear you give *lip service*, but not real customer service? Do they interpret you to mean *"Do what I say, not what I do"?* If so, you have a serious problem. And only you can fix it.

> *"A POWERFUL LEADER IS NOT FOUND BEFORE OR BEHIND THE TEAM. SHE MAKES HER PLACE BESIDE THEM."*

What kind of 'role models' do your people really see?		
Our leaders say one thing, but do another. It's NATO around here: 'No Action, Talk Only'.	Our managers are helpful when we meet the revenue targets. If not, look out!	My boss *lives* the company values. I'm inspired to work with leaders who really mean it.
1 .... 2 .... 3 .... 4 5		

www.RonKaufman.com

15. The question of *empowerment*

How much authority should you grant to frontline workers? How much leeway should new staff be given? At what point can your workers make an immediate decision? When must they check with the boss or get approval from their manager or supervisor?

Where does authority reside in your organization? Where does real decision making happen? Is it at the top of the pyramid, close to the Head Office? Or have you driven this power close to the frontline, close to the action, close to your customer's concerns?

Does it take a long time for your organization to make a firm decision? And if the decision yields poor results, does it take forever to make a new one?

At the **Ritz Carlton Hotel**, employees have the authority to waive charges on a guest's bill to help resolve an upsetting situation. New staff soon learn what amounts are appropriate and effective. They are empowered to act quickly, not just forward the problem to someone else.

At the **Service Quality Centre**, the first General Manager told all the staff, *"You have the authority. Make a decision and take action for your customers. Just don't bankrupt the company. And trust me, this company won't go bankrupt."*

What about your team? Are they supported by a culture of *empowerment*, or are they mired in bureaucracy with no freedom to move, stuck and unable to serve?

Are your people empowered?		
Sure, we can make decisions. But if we're wrong, we're dead.	Do what you see the bosses do. In the future, just follow the past.	We can use our common sense. We do what's best for the customer.
1 2	.... 3 4	 5

When culture nourishes, service flourishes

Your company culture is like water. It can flow strongly and steadily, refreshing your team and carrying people forward. Or it can sit festering and stagnant, gradually poisoning those around it.

It can be fertile and rich, irrigating growth and stimulating new ideas. Or it can be destructive and narrow, crashing down upon any signs of change.

Nourish your people. Encourage ideas. Reward what works. Inspire new learning and celebrate success. Create an *UP Your Service!* culture.

> *"THE THING THAT LIES AT THE FOUNDATION*
> *OF POSITIVE CHANGE, THE WAY I SEE IT,*
> *IS SERVICE TO A FELLOW HUMAN BEING."*
>
> LECH WALESA

What's your total score for an *UP Your Service!* culture?

Your score	Ron's recommendation
1 - 19	Your culture is dead or dying. You need fresh air, quick!
20 - 39	Nothing special here. Your staff can be easily poached away.
40 - 59	A strong culture that supports the right ideas. Keep it growing.
60 - 75	A great place to work for staff and customers, too! Well done!

How do you get more bananas?

Put five monkeys in a cage. Put a ladder in the cage with a bunch of bananas at the top. As soon as one monkey starts to climb the ladder, spray cold water on all the monkeys. When another tries to climb, spray cold water on all the monkeys again. Soon, no monkey will attempt to climb the ladder.

Now remove one monkey and put a new monkey in the cage. The new monkey will see the bananas and try to climb the ladder. Not wanting to be sprayed with cold water again, the other monkeys will quickly pull him down.

Remove a second monkey and put a new monkey in the cage. Again, the new monkey will see the bananas and try to climb the ladder. Not wanting to be sprayed with cold water, the other monkeys will quickly pull him down.

Repeat this process until all five original monkeys are gone, and five new monkeys are in the cage. None will try to climb the ladder, and none will understand why.

Now remove all five monkeys and put a brand new monkey in the cage. The monkey will quickly climb the ladder and eat the bananas. Don't spray any cold water.

Put the five original monkeys back in the cage with the one brand new monkey who has tasted the delicious bananas.

Replenish the bananas.

The brand new monkey will again climb up the ladder. Despite the efforts of the older monkeys to hold him down, the brand new monkey has tasted the bananas; he will strive again until he succeeds.

When he does succeed, the other five monkeys will realize that bananas are worth the climb, and worth the risk of some cold water. They, too, will climb the ladder and enjoy the delicious bananas.

What's the moral of the story?

- A little *cold water* can destroy a lot of motivation. Be careful your management team does not *spray*.

- Fear of group punishment will hold back individual initiative. If an individual makes a mistake, don't make the whole group suffer (unless you are intentionally harnessing peer pressure to encourage uniformity of action).

- New staff will tend to take on the behavioral characteristics of your existing team members. Therefore, be sure your new hires are coached and mentored by the best of your existing team.

- Fresh perspective is important to continue growth and success. Bring in new staff with new ideas from time to time. Rotate existing staff to new departments or positions.

- Trying something new can yield delicious rewards. To encourage initiative and risk-taking in your organization, keep replenishing the bananas.

What additional insights do you see? What moral of the story can you add?

What would *you* do?

Your company's service vision was written long ago. It no longer motivates, connects or inspires. You have been tasked with rewriting the vision to bring it up to date. How will you go about this important project?

Turnover amongst new staff is unacceptably high. A large percentage of new hires leave the company within six months. What changes can you make to your recruitment and orientation programs to improve this situation?

What is the most popular training program in your company? Why? What do people say about it? Which is the least popular or effective? How do you suggest changing it?

Your Employee of the Month campaign has become a popularity contest. Some say it's just an ongoing political effort by the Human Resources Department. You need to replace it with something more appropriate and inspiring. What do you have in mind? Where can you get some more good ideas?

A panel discussion is planned to bring management and staff closer together. You are afraid no staff will speak up, and management might speak down. What can you do before and during the event to encourage a candid meeting in the middle?

One of your managers is brilliant, but dictatorial and gruff. Your job is to enroll him in supporting a culture change program. How will you gain his participation?

"UP Your Service! requires good decisions every day. It's up to you!"

UP Your Service! action steps

Read through the recruitment section in your newspaper. Which advertisements sound intriguing? Which are most believable? Cut them out and paste them on the wall. Put your advertisements side-by-side. How do yours compare?

List ten ways to attract and recruit new staff. Which are most effective? How many does your organization use today? Which of these could be most beneficial in your future?

Close your eyes. From memory, repeat your organization's service vision. In your own words, explain what it means. What percentage of your staff can complete this exercise?

Study the service vision of your best competitors. What differentiates you from them? How can you make that clear?

Talk to your newest staff members. Ask them for two suggestions to improve the Orientation Program. Implement immediately.

Improve your housekeeping now. List five things that can be done within five days to make your space look brighter, cleaner and more service-focused. Do all five, then list five more.

Make a list of community causes. Include sports, the arts, education, environment, minorities and the disadvantaged. From the company's point of view, what are the pros and cons of supporting each?

Write a thoughtful letter or an article about creating and sustaining a strong service culture. Publish it in your hometown newspaper, company newsletter or on your website.

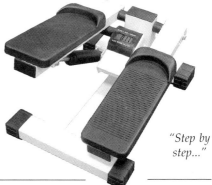

"Step by step..."

5

UP Your Service!
Standards

*If you want to succeed and grow, you must achieve
high standards in four essential categories.*

*First, you must create excellent **products** and **services**.*

*Second, you need terrific **delivery systems** to keep track
and get the products to your customers on time.*

*Third, you have to attract and keep great staff
with a winning **service mindset**.*

*And fourth, you must build long-term **customer
relationships** that endure and mature over time.*

*In each category, how good are you now,
and how good do you need to be?*

*What does it take to keep your customers happy,
and keep them coming back for more?*

*Is it enough to be average? Just like all the others?
Or do you need to reach UP higher?*

*And if so, **how high**?*

Criminal belongs in jail!

CRIMINAL

Criminal is so bad, it violates minimum expectations. This is the taxi driver with a lousy attitude driving a vehicle with broken headlights who thinks he's competing for first place in the demolition derby! It's the guy who says, *"I'll call you back this afternoon"*, and never bothers to call; the bank with errors on your monthly statement; the website screaming *"Order Now! Satisfaction Guaranteed!"*…but they never acknowledge, process or reply to your order.

Now look carefully at your people and your business. Are *you* in violation?

Criminal products and services

- The product is defective upon arrival, or stops working shortly after purchase. The telephone doesn't work. The food is rancid. The hotel toilet overflows. The car won't start.

- The product scratches, leaks or explodes. It damages other products, people and professional reputations. The new software package contains a virus. The insect repellent causes rashes. The furniture polish strips off the finish.

- The advertised price disguises the true cost of ownership.

Criminal delivery systems

- The right product is delivered to the wrong person or to the wrong location, or is never delivered at all!

- The wrong product is delivered to the right person; too many, not enough, incorrect size, wrong style, different color, outdated version or obsolete model.

- The installation is done badly, causing damage or delay.

Criminal service mindsets

- Staff are rude, crude, arrogant, ignorant, insulting or offensive. They laugh at customers who don't understand, and humiliate those with problems. They complain loudly about their jobs, their colleagues and customers.

Criminal relationships

- The company pretends to be interested in long-term business, but takes action only for immediate profits.

- The company lies, cheats or steals from the customer, or shares proprietary information with your competition.

Basic is the bare minimum

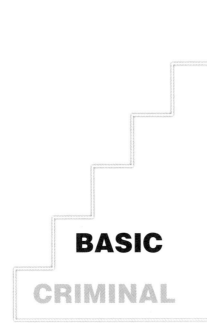

BASIC

CRIMINAL

Basic is so disappointing. This is the taxi driver with a smelly car who gets lost on the way to your destination. He makes no conversation, no apology and no effort to help you with your bags. This is the newspaper delivered wet; the restaurant that is sold out on the one thing you really want to order; the waiter who forgets to bring your dessert and your change at the end of the meal. This is the fitness club with not enough shower rooms and no hot water.

What about your people and your business? Are you disappointing?

Basic products and services

- The product is outdated, almost obsolete. It works, but doesn't have any of the latest features or improvements.

- The product comes with instructions that are too technical, complex or simply not enough. You struggle to get results.

- The product is overpriced. The discount is a sham.

Basic delivery systems

- The product arrives in multiple packages which come at different times. It takes a while to get all the pieces together.

- The product arrives damaged from the shipment: torn, scratched or dented. The delivery folks leave you to file your own report for replacement or compensation.

- The installation takes much longer than expected. It is obvious the technicians are amateurs using your project for on-the-job training. They leave your place in a mess.

Basic service mindsets

- The staff clearly don't care about you. In fact, they don't care much about *anything* except leaving work and getting paid.

- The staff have no clear understanding of the products or company procedures. They are untrained and immature.

Basic relationships

- The company makes no effort to appreciate you for your business. They think they are doing you a favor.

- The company leaves your personal order information in clear view for other staff and customers to see.

Expected is just the average

Expected is nothing special. It's the average, the usual, the norm. This is the taxi driver who knows the address but makes no effort to welcome you to town. It's the train that arrives on time. It's the photographer who takes your passport photo but does nothing to adjust the lighting. This is the museum with artifacts but no engaging narrative or unusual exhibits. It's the website that welcomes your order, but *only* if you live in the USA.

Are you doing the same as everyone else? Are you nothing more than *expected*?

Expected products and services

- The product does what it is supposed to do. It performs according to standard specifications.

- The product is properly packaged and the instructions are clear. Questions are answered by studying the operating instructions or the enclosed user's manual.

- The price is on par with the industry average. No special terms are offered or allowed.

Expected delivery systems

- The correct product arrives at the right location, at the right time.

- The delivery personnel are efficient. They know how to handle installation without any problems.

Expected service mindsets

- The staff make eye contact and say *"Hello"* when they greet you. On the telephone, they identify themselves by company and by name.

- Staff say *"Thank you"* at the end of your transaction. They are willing to help if you have questions.

Expected relationships

- The company keeps track of who you are and what you've purchased. If you have any questions in the future, they will be able to review your order.

- If you are a big customer, the company sends you a holiday card at the end of the year.

Desired is what people hope for!

DESIRED

EXPECTED

BASIC

CRIMINAL

Desired is something special. This is the taxi driver with a friendly greeting and a warm smile. He knows the best way to get around traffic. His car is clean and he gladly helps you with your bags. This is the doctor with a good bedside manner. It's the Post Office staff who patiently explains three ways you can ship your parcel. This is the sales staff at the clothing store who helps you select colors and styles to improve your professional image.

This is what people hope for. Is this what you and your team are providing?

Desired products and services

- The product works even better than expected. There are new features and benefits you find very useful.

- The user's guide is easy to read and understand. The company's website has up-to-date information to help you get maximum value from your purchase.

- The price is good value, just below the industry average.

Desired delivery systems

- The company pre-arranges a date for delivery that is most convenient for you. The delivery team arrives on time.

- The delivery team is well-groomed and very polite. They congratulate you on your purchase and patiently answer any questions.

- The crew makes a good effort to clean up, dispose of packaging materials and restore your home or office to new or spotless condition.

Desired service mindsets

- Staff show genuine appreciation. They remember your name and welcome you personally when you visit. On the telephone, they use your name often in the conversation.

- Staff sincerely thank you for your business. If you have a question, they are happy to assist you.

Desired relationships

- The company proactively contacts you to make sure you are pleased with your past purchases. They suggest new products and services to help you achieve greater value.

Surprising is leading the field!

SURPRISING

DESIRED

EXPECTED

BASIC

CRIMINAL

Surprising is a WOW! This is the taxi driver who knows the scenic way, the shortest way and the fastest way to reach your destination. He explains all three and asks which you prefer. He offers you today's newspaper and a pleasant choice of music. This is the circus clown who brings audience members up on stage; the hotel that always remembers your favorite food and drinks (**Le Meridien Hotel** in Dubai remembers mine!); the school that makes extraordinary efforts to customize lessons for your child.

This is what people remember and rave about to others. Do they rave about you?

Surprising products and services

- The product does much more than expected. It is easily upgraded and is compatible with other products and services in the market.

- The product opens unexpected possibilities. The support materials and interactive website help you find new ways to get more value from your purchase.

- The price is a real bargain, with excellent and flexible terms.

Surprising delivery systems

- Delivery team members are well-trained customer support specialists. They install quickly, clean perfectly and provide a maintenance check on existing products without charge.

- You are given detailed instructions on how to contact the company anytime during the day or night.

Surprising service mindsets

- The staff know you well and they understand your business. They compliment you on your achievements and suggest new ideas to help you continue your success.

- Staff are delighted to answer your questions. They seek your recommendations on how to make instructional materials more user-friendly and effective.

- Staff enthusiasm proves infectious. You contact the company regularly simply because they boost your day.

Surprising relationships

- The company is committed to your long-term success. They include you in focus groups to help design new products.

Unbelievable is truly world class!

UNBELIEVABLE!

SURPRISING

DESIRED

EXPECTED

BASIC

CRIMINAL

Unbelievable is astonishingly great! This taxi driver is truly enthusiastic. He is living his service mission. His spotless vehicle has a pleasant fragrance and fresh, moist towels for your comfort. He has a wide assortment of great music, current newspapers and reading materials. At the end of the ride he brings your bags to the doorstep and hands you a business card with his photograph, name and telephone number. On the back is a handwritten note: *"Thank you for being my customer. Have a terrific day!"*

These are the legends of spectacular service! Can you and your colleagues achieve it?

Unbelievable products and services

- The product is extraordinary, producing results far beyond anything you've experienced in the past.

- The product comes with an extra upgrade at no charge, plus a lifetime supply of parts, add-ons and other materials.

- The price is a once-in-a-lifetime special. You love it!

Unbelievable delivery systems

- The product arrives and automatically installs itself while simultaneously upgrading, maintaining and fine-tuning the environment around it.

- The delivery team go all the way to produce an exceptional customer experience. They are entertaining and educational, leaving you in a fabulous mood to face the future.

Unbelievable service mindsets

- Staff regularly exceed all customer expectations. They constantly seek ways to surprise and delight you.

- Key staff members are dedicated to personally support and manage your relationship with the company. Over time they become your friends and confidants. They earn it.

Unbelievable relationships

- The company provides an ongoing value-added service to understand your changing needs and provide you with exceptionally well-suited products.

- You are only charged for what produces practical and valuable results. There is no risk to you, while your complete satisfaction is 100% guaranteed.

Where are *you* and *your company* today?

Take a close look.

What are the standards of your organization?

How good are your products and services?

How reliable and user-friendly are your delivery systems?

How warm and welcoming is the service mindset of your staff?

How well do you cultivate long-term relationships with your customers?

CRIMINAL	**BASIC**	**EXPECTED**
In violation of the basic norms.	Only doing the bare minimum.	Just meets the usual standards.

Where are *your competitors* today?

Now take another look.

What are the standards of your best competitors?

Are their products and services better than yours?

Are their delivery systems easier to use, more streamlined, more reliable?

Which competitor has the best reputation for patient and helpful service staff?

Who builds longer term relationships with customers? You, or your competition?

DESIRED	**SURPRISING**	**UNBELIEVABLE**
Appreciated and respected.	Innovative. Unique.	Extraordinary. Astonishing.
Really good!	*Delightful!*	*The very best!*

What would *you* do?

Two companies are merging into a single organization. One has built a premium reputation for impeccable customer care. The other is known as a firm that delivers the basics, but nothing more. Your job is two-fold:

1. *How will you integrate and align the staff of both companies? How will you keep the premium staff motivated and on-board? How will you get the basic staff to raise their service standards?*

2. *The process of integration will take some time. What message will you send to your customers and suppliers? How will you manage their expectations during the transition?*

One motivated staff member delivers consistently unbelievable service. Customers are so enthusiastic they refuse to be served by any other staff. This is causing a problem in scheduling, and could turn into a problem for staff morale. *How will you handle this situation? How can you turn this to everyone's advantage?*

A complaint about your service is published in the local newspaper. You know the situation was highly unusual, caused by a combination of internal and external factors. Your job is to reply to the customer personally and to write a reply for the newspaper. *How would you handle each situation? Would you say anything differently to the customer and to newspaper readers?*

"UP Your Service! means caring about your customers, your staff and everyone around you. It takes a strong commitment!"

UP Your Service! action steps

When you go out this week, keep track of which service inter-actions truly delight you. As you shop, dine, purchase, travel, ask questions or do errands, notice how each service provider uses, or loses, the opportunity to give you a higher level of service.

Make the effort to acknowledge excellent service. Write compliments. Leave tips. Let the people know you *appreciate* their service.

Use the *Yellow Pages* to gather information over the telephone. Research a new technology, service or installation. Take notes on each call. Rate the tone of voice, choice of language, depth of product knowledge, and overall helpful-ness, flexibility and responsiveness of the staff.

What makes one conversation more satisfying than another? What stands out in your mind as a *surprising* level of telephone service? Compile your results. Share them with everyone who uses the telephone in your organization. *(And that's everyone!)*

Excellent service standards are S.M.A.R.T.:

S - specific, clear and precise, not vague
M - measurable, quantifiable, objective
A - achievable, a stretch but not impossible
R - relevant to customers
T - time-bound, a clear date for
        achievement

Now check *your* quality service standards. Are they SMART enough to meet this standard?

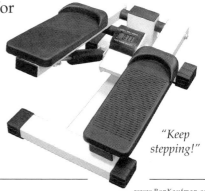

"Keep stepping!"

CHAPTER

6

UP Your Service!
Interactions

*Every connection with a business, customer or
colleague exists in a spectrum
of time and depth.*

*Some interactions are temporary and shallow.
They are fleeting, short-lived, over in an instant.
I call these interactions **one-shot deals**.*

*Other interactions take longer, involving more
moments of participation, decision or reflection.
These can lead to **transaction satisfaction**.*

*In certain cases, the interaction doesn't really end.
It carries on consistently and predictably over time.
These become our dependable and
reliable relationships.*

*And in special circumstances, the interaction
not only continues over time, but magnifies in
importance and value for everyone involved.
These are the **powerful partnerships** in our lives.*

Take a closer look. Where on this spectrum are you?

The one-shot deal

You are walking down the street. On the side of the road is a table with magazines and newspapers for sale. You buy a newspaper and walk away. You've just had a *one-shot deal.*

In a one-shot deal, *what you see is what you get.* You have to *take it or leave it.* The vendor may be *here today, but gone tomorrow.* And let's include *'caveat emptor': let the buyer beware!* since there is no promise or guarantee about the future.

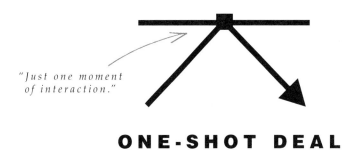

"Just one moment of interaction."

ONE-SHOT DEAL

In a one-shot deal there is only one relatively short moment of interaction. Here are some examples:

- Meet an attractive person at a party, but drift apart before you get a chance to agree on another time to meet.

- Exchange foreign currency at a "bureau de change" in a European city you rarely visit.

- Buy equipment on sale at an inventory clearance sale. The terms are strictly "Cash & Carry. All sales are final."

- Buy used goods at auction without the original guarantees. Items are bought and sold as is. **eBay** and other auction sites grow by enabling these one-shot interactions.

Transaction satisfaction

You are thirsty. At the grocery store, the electric door opens with an impressive *swoosh*. The lighting is good, the air conditioning cool, the music upbeat and there is a pleasant odor in the air. The juice section is well stocked with a variety of fresh and reasonably priced drinks. At the checkout, the cashier gives you a drinking straw, a nice smile and the correct change.

You've just experienced *transaction satisfaction.*

"Multiple perception points."

TRANSACTION SATISFACTION

In a transaction, many perception points or 'moments of truth' occur where quality of service is assessed. For example:

- On a date with a new friend, you are aware of what to wear, where to eat, which movie to see, what to talk about, and what to do *after* the movie.

- Purchase clothing at a retail store like **Nordstrom** and you notice the decor, fashions, colors, prices, helpfulness of the staff, giftwrapping service, availability and skill of alterations.

- Fly on an airline like **United** and you will evaluate the ease of reservations, price of tickets, speed of check-in, size and spacing of the seats, quality of food and in-flight entertainment, baggage handling, on-time departure and arrival.

Reliable relationships

Buy a book, music or video at **Amazon.com**. The next time you visit, the site will welcome you back by name. Want to order again? The company remembers what you bought last time (and will recommend others like it), your credit card number (and will verify it), your shipping address (and will confirm it) and what method of shipment you chose the last time around. Everything is ready for your selection. You can order with just one click. That's a *reliable relationship.*

"The interaction continues, time and time again."

RELIABLE RELATIONSHIPS

In reliable relationships, both parties prove themselves to be dependable, reliable and consistent. These are the people and companies you can count on, time and time again. For example:

- Enjoy a long-term relationship with someone you really admire. Build your trust and mutual affection over time.

- Open an account with **DHL**, **Federal Express**, **UPS** or **TNT**. All of them will give you guaranteed delivery, regular pick-ups, reliable billing and steady customer service.

- Order newspaper delivery from a reliable vendor. The paper will be on your doorstep at the same time every morning regardless of the weather. When it rains, the paper will be inside your screen door. Snows? It's in a plastic bag.

Powerful partnerships

You open a new office. The manager of a nearby stationery store stops by to welcome you and learn more about your business. She offers to coordinate your printing needs and replenish your office supplies at competitive prices, provide customized in-office delivery and open a credit account. She agrees to stock an item you need that is not usually on her shelves and makes useful local referrals to help you in your business. This is the beginning of a *powerful partnership*.

"The interaction grows more valuable...for both sides."

POWERFUL PARTNERSHIPS

In a powerful partnership, both parties obtain greater *value* over time. The partnership becomes more important, positive, productive, prosperous, profitable and proactive. For example:

- Create a loving home, raise children, take care of each other in sickness and in health, grow old and happy together.

- **One World** and **Star Alliance** improve airline service to customers through code sharing and other collaborations. Customer loyalty to the airlines increases.

- Great staff see their careers grow with ongoing support from the company. The company enjoys greater benefit from increasingly talented and well-trained staff. It's a win–win–win for the employees, company and customers.

More examples of service interactions

A customer calls for a price quote over the phone. You call back with the amount.

A stranger asks for directions.

Someone stops by and wants to use the restroom.

A person buys something from you. You explain its use, wrap the purchase and collect payment. You keep the interaction friendly and make sure your products and storefront are looking good.

ONE-SHOT DEAL

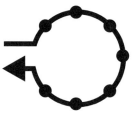

TRANSACTION SATISFACTION

At the open market, you walk through rows and aisles of spices, candies, fresh fruits, garments, toys and household goods. By the time you leave, your arms are full.

Back home, one item doesn't fit right and two things don't work as they should. But it's pointless to take them back. You don't remember where you bought them and the vendor won't remember you!

The teams at **Disneyland** and **Walt Disney World** polish every perception point to perfection. The grounds are spotless and staff are friendly. The characters are real every moment. The rides are safe, food is good, and information is provided quickly. Souvenirs are plentiful, too!

You spend a lot in just one day, but have no regrets at all. The experience was terrific!

Which interactions are *you* doing?

A repeat customer opens an account with you. You supply them with standard products and services on a regular basis. You invoice them monthly and they always pay on time.

You learn more about your customers' business and design new services to meet their unique needs. They are willing to pay premium prices and increase order volume over time.

RELIABLE RELATIONSHIPS

POWERFUL PARTNERSHIPS

Regular customers at the **Sheraton Towers** experience a superior level of care. The concierge knows your name. Your favorite fruits are up in your room, your choice of newspaper already provided. Laundry recalls you prefer no starch. Room service notes your preference for warm milk before you go to sleep.

It's just the way you like it. It happens every time.

In Korea, **MasterCard** is building a strong partnership with a chip manufacturer, bank, telephone company, university and government agency to make one card for students that is their charge card, cash card, phone card, student card, library card and identity card all in one.

In turn, students use the card more often and buy more with it. Good for MasterCard!

What would *you* do?

A new employee wants to fast track his career. He asks you to mentor him with guidance, advice and helpful information. He knows a good mentor relationship is mutually beneficial, and asks what he can do to help you. *What is your reply?*

Your doctor sends you an article from a medical journal about a topic of interest to you. You never asked her for it, she simply took the initiative to mail you a copy or send you the website address. You'd like to return the favor. *What can you do for your doctor that will make her life better?*

One of your partners has decided to retire. Two other people offer to make an investment and take over the vacant position. The original partnership evolved over many years of trial and error. *How would you work with these two new partners to shorten the learning curve and optimize your chances of success?*

A new supplier enters the market. He promises high quality, fast delivery, great service and low price. He asks for an order from your business. Another supplier you've worked with for years cautions you against giving the fellow a try. *What would you do in this situation?*

Transactions are over when completed, but relationships go on and on. *What can you do to extend business transactions into the future? How can you keep your customers coming back again and again?*

"A tough situation arises. The team looks to you for good ideas and guidance."

UP Your Service! action steps

Make a list of ten suppliers to your business. Identify which style of interaction you currently have with each. Which are *one-shot deals?* Who provides *transaction satisfaction?* Where are you in *reliable relationships?* Are you enjoying any truly *powerful partnerships?*

Which of these supplier interactions could be *upgraded* to the next level? What advantages would changing the interaction bring to you and your organization? What actions can you take to start the process?

Powerful partnership **is not appropriate for all your interactions.** Sometimes a one-shot deal is all you want or need. But that doesn't mean they are any less useful. The next time you pick up a newspaper, ride a bus or buy an ice-cream cone, be sure to *thank* the service provider. It may be just a one-shot deal, but it's still a human to human interaction.

Choose two departments in your organization. How can they work more closely together to improve their interactions? Can they reduce errors or reduce costs? Could they increase speed, accuracy or innovation? Have a conversation with the head of both departments. Get the project going.

Consider your personal life. Think about your spouse, children, parents, siblings, friends and colleagues.

For each person on your list, write down three ways they enrich your life and three things you can do to touch theirs. Now do them!

"Step, step, step!"

7

Explore, Agree, Deliver, Assure

To build a reputation for UP Your Service!,
you must go beyond the momentary one-shot deal.

You must cultivate expertise in
providing transaction satisfaction,
creating reliable relationships and
building powerful partnerships into the future.

These styles of interaction are all circular in nature.

They are characterized by completed **service cycles***.*

Each service cycle is a series of interconnected conversations:
explore*,* ***agree****,* ***deliver*** *and* ***assure****.*

Not every service provider does a good job in all four areas.
In fact, most are chronically weak in at least one.

Read this chapter carefully. Take the test at the end.

Where are you already strong?
Where should you improve to UP Your Service!?

Understand each other: *explore*

Explore

Build awareness, rapport and mutual understanding.

What is valuable? What is possible? What can we invent or do together?

Learn more about your prospects, colleagues and customers. Help them learn more about you.

1. Explore

2. Agree

3. Deliver

4. Assure

Speculate. Discover. Generate new possibilities and fresh ideas.

What do you want? What do you need? What are your hopes and dreams? Is there a budget, a timeline, a limit on your resources? How will you recognize and measure success? In business, these questions are associated with *marketing*.

Make clear promises: *agree*

Explore

Build awareness, rapport and mutual understanding.

What is valuable? What is possible? What can we invent or do together?

Learn more about your prospects, colleagues and customers. Help them learn more about you.

Agree

Negotiate constructively. Establish clear terms and conditions. Make mutual promises you can keep.

What will we do for each other? By when, where, how?

Find the common ground where all parties are motivated to succeed.

Make beneficial promises and commitments. Develop contingency plans.

What are your standards for performance, delivery and fulfillment. How will we track progress and keep in touch? If things don't go as expected, what is our contingency plan? In business, these are the concerns of *production planning* and *sales.*

Do what you promise: *deliver*

Explore

Build awareness, rapport and mutual understanding.

What is valuable? What is possible? What can we invent or do together?

Learn more about your prospects, colleagues and customers. Help them learn more about you.

Agree

Negotiate constructively. Establish clear terms and conditions. Make mutual promises you can keep.

What will we do for each other? By when, where, how?

Find the common ground where all parties are motivated to succeed.

Execution is key. Dedicate adequate resources. Get the job done correctly the first time around.

Deliver

Do what you promised to do. Produce, create, manufacture, pack, ship, install, test, train, upgrade, modify, customize, invoice, collect..and serve.

Track your agreements. If breakdowns occur, use your agreed contingency plans.

Are we keeping our promises? Are we on schedule? Do we need more or fewer resources? If there are unexpected difficulties, have we kept the right people well-informed? In business, these issues are addressed by *manufacturing, operations* and *logistics*.

Confirm satisfaction: *assure*

Explore

Build awareness, rapport and mutual understanding.

What is valuable? What is possible? What can we invent or do together?

Learn more about your prospects, colleagues and customers. Help them learn more about you.

Agree

Negotiate constructively. Establish clear terms and conditions. Make mutual promises you can keep.

What will we do for each other? By when, where, how?

Find the common ground where all parties are motivated to succeed.

Confirm client and partner satisfaction. Find ways to improve for the next time.

Assure

Make sure all parties are fully satisfied with the results. If not, explore what needs to be done.

Seek ways to do better. Review what did not go according to plan. For future projects, revise the plan or change the standards for fulfillment.

Deliver

Do what you promised to do. Produce, create, manufacture, pack, ship, install, test, train, upgrade, modify, customize, invoice, collect..and serve.

Track your agreements. If breakdowns occur, use your agreed contingency plans.

Have we fulfilled our promises? Are you satisfied with the results? Do you have suggestions on how we can deliver an even better job next time? What else should we review together? In business, this is the domain of *after-sales customer service*.

How thoroughly do you *explore?*

- Do you *truly* understand the concerns and needs of your customers, colleagues and prospects?

- Are your people skilled at creating rapport, comfort and dialog with others? Do they know how to interview and ask questions without being pushy?

- Can your staff educate prospective customers about your products and services without appearing *'hard sell'?*

- Do you *eagerly* seek and create new possibilities? Are you open to *'out of the box'* brainstorming? Will you consider fresh and untested ideas?

- How *quickly* and *easily* can someone locate detailed and up-to-date information about you, your services and your organization?

How completely do you *assure?*

- Are you consistently *'closing the loop'* and following up to ensure client and partner satisfaction?

- Do you have a proven system for gathering candid feedback from your customers?

- Do you have a mechanism for capturing and leveraging customer preferences, compliments and complaints?

- Are your interactions with customers consistently growing in size, importance and value?

- Does your customer base provide you with enthusiastic and effective referrals?

How readily do you *agree?*

- Is your organization genuinely flexible, user-friendly and *'easy to do business with'?*

- How accommodating are you with your terms, timelines and conditions?

- Can customers easily customize, tailor and fine-tune what you have to offer? Do you make it convenient for them to have it the way they want it?

  - Are your agreements with customers clearly documented in language that is easy to understand?

    - Do you make comprehensive and effective contingency plans? Are these plans reviewed and updated regularly with your customers and your colleagues?

How consistently do you *deliver?*

- How often do you do things right the *first* time?

- How solid is your reputation for accurate, dependable and reliable products and services?

- Do you have an excellent system for tracking orders, production and deliveries? Are your clients and colleagues updated regularly?

- Are people and resources automatically reassigned to projects requiring extra or immediate attention?

- If problems occur and things do not go according to plan, how quickly are the right people notified? How soon before your contingency plans take over?

Benchmarking Amazon.com

Amazon.com is a highly successful retail site on the Internet. Amazon.com started as a bookstore with millions of titles and now has *billions* of dollars in market capitalization.

How does Amazon.com help you *explore*?

- Search by any topic or title. Amazon.com shows you related titles, other titles by the same author, and titles of books purchased by people who also purchased this book.

- Amazon.com provides book reviews from other readers as well as the publisher and author.

- If you are a member of a specific community, company or affinity group, Amazon.com can tell you what books people in that group are buying now.

How does Amazon.com *assure*?

- Amazon.com is committed to your complete satisfaction. If you have a problem, they will reply to you quickly by e-mail and take remedial actions right away. I once received a book that was slightly dirty. They sent me a replacement at no charge, overnight.

- You can track your orders in process and see your complete order history at any time. You can change your address, password or billing information whenever you wish.

- If you have any suggestions to help improve the service, Amazon.com enthusiastically welcomes your ideas.

Amazon.com is not just a bookstore. It now offers a wide range of books, music, videos, electronics, toys, auctions and more.

How does Amazon.com do it?

Amazon.com earns high levels of customer satisfaction with every purchase and builds extraordinary levels of loyalty. It's quite straightforward: they *explore, agree, deliver* and *assure!*

How does Amazon.com *agree*?

- You can have products sent to multiple locations, request individual giftwrapping (and choose the style of paper), pay either by credit card, wire transfer or check.

  - You can choose standard, express or overnight delivery and see the costs of each before deciding. If a product is not in stock, you can have each item sent as it becomes available, or hold and ship all your items at once. If you choose the first option, Amazon.com guarantees shipping costs will be no more than if you chose the second.

How does Amazon.com *deliver*?

  - As soon as you place an order, you receive an e-mail confirming all the details. You can change it if you reply right away.

  - When your order is filled, you get another confirmation by e-mail. Your credit card is charged only when the order is actually shipped.

- Products are packed in strong boxes with extra padding to ensure they reach you in new condition.

- Inside each box is a complete description of the order and an attractive bookmark or other information or gift.

Amazon.com accumulates the trust of loyal customers around the world. This company is bound for profit and success.

Planning your wedding

Explore

Should the wedding be inside, outdoors, large or small, in the morning, evening or afternoon? What are the religious and official marriage requirements? Gather ideas from friends, hotels, websites and magazines. Dream about your honeymoon trip and wedding gifts.

Agree

Prepare the guest list. Choose the venue. Confirm the menu, table decorations and music. Prepare the seating arrangements. Agree upon all costs. Book your honeymoon vacation. File your wish list with a gift registry. Manage the stress. Keep on dreaming.

Assure

Send *Thank You* cards to guests and family members. Give feedback to the service providers: hotel, caterer and musicians. Copy and frame the photographs. Be grateful. Renew your vows each day. Make your dreams come true.

Deliver

Send out the invitations. Buy the dress. Wrap warm blankets around your cold feet. Sign the papers, say the vows, be sure you really mean it. Exchange rings, kiss the groom or the bride, dance with your in-laws. Live your dreams now!

A great wedding starts long before the music plays and the bride and groom say *"I do"*. Use this set of reminders to plan your next social event, party or celebration.

Upgrading a computer network

Explore

What problems are you experiencing with the current configuration? What new technologies do you plan to use or install in the future? What existing systems must be maintained? Who should be involved in the planning? How soon is this required?

Agree

Determine the new system requirements. Select vendors to do the job. Establish hardware and software specifications. Agree upon project budgets and milestones. Confirm service level agreements. Commit internal resources to support and track the project.

Assure

Gather feedback from users. Send bug reports and system difficulties to the vendors for rapid resolution. Give comments to trainers to improve future courses. Conduct post-project reviews to enhance future upgrades.

Deliver

Install new equipment. Debug the installation with beta-testing. Run parallel systems until cut-over, or gradually migrate existing users to the new configuration. Provide training to ensure the users gain maximum value.

Computer upgrades can be trouble if not prepared well in advance. Use this sequence of key conversations to make your upgrade smooth and efficient for everyone.

Buying insurance

Explore

Talk about insurance with friends and family members. Meet and interview different insurance agents and brokers. Surf the web for more useful information. Read articles on the pros and cons of various insurance policies. Ask questions about riders, waivers and exclusions.

Agree

Decide if you need protection or investment; life, health, property, liability or disability? How much coverage and for how long? Compare policies and payment options. Choose a plan and select appropriate riders. Confirm details with your agent, broker or company.

Assure

Conduct an annual review of your existing insurance coverage, considering new options, policies and regulations. Stay in touch with your insurance company, agent or broker. Ask questions as they arise. Enjoy the birthday card.

Deliver

Complete the forms. Get a medical check-up. Review policy documents for accuracy. Include the policy in your will if appropriate. File claims as required. Send in your premium payments on time. Rest assured, you are covered.

Buying insurance can be confusing, even scary, for many people. Find an agent or broker who follows these guidelines to help you make a comfortable and constructive decision.

Selling insurance

Explore

Understand your company's policies and products. Ask your prospect insightful questions. Listen carefully to understand your prospect's wants and needs. Explain how you have assisted other clients with similar opportunities, concerns or situations.

Agree

Identify appropriate policies for your client. Give a friendly and complete presentation. Help your client make a positive, practical decision. Answer any questions about the contract in user-friendly language. Confirm the date for your client's medical check-up.

Assure

Meet regularly with clients to review needs and insurance coverage. Gather and provide timely information about changes and new opportunities. Remember birthdays and anniversaries. Ask for good referrals.

Deliver

Collect the application form and first premium. Deliver the policy when issued with a complete review of all the terms and conditions. Provide claim forms and assist with filing if required. Send a thank-you note.

Selling insurance can be rewarding if you build a reputation for superior service and get enthusiastic referrals every year. Use these proven steps to make it happen.

Hiring new team members

Explore

What position needs to be filled? What expertise is required? When is the new person needed? How will candidates be evaluated? Who should be involved in the selection process? Will you promote someone from within, or look for new talent from outside?

Agree

What are the responsibilities of this position? What is the level of authority? How will performance be appraised? How will remuneration be determined? Who will these people work with, supervise and report to? Where will they be located? When will they get started?

Assure

Get input from superiors, sub-ordinates, peers, customers and sup-pliers. Give feedback to new team members to encourage learning and help increase effectiveness. Ask new team members for ideas to improve the recruitment process.

Deliver

Hire the new staff. Announce the appointment. Prepare an effective orientation program. Assign tasks and resources for the job. Create opportunities for new and existing staff to interact, share, learn and grow together quickly.

Selecting new staff is a huge responsibility. Include your colleagues in the process from the beginning. Use these action steps to start out right and build a winning team.

Building trust is a four-step process

Each time you *explore, agree, deliver* and *assure,* the possibility for **trust** grows between you and the other person. In fact, this may be the only way human beings can *build trust* with one another.

1. Find out what is important to the other person.
2. Make a promise to do something on their behalf.
3. Do what you promised.
4. Check and make sure they are satisfied.

Completed
cycles build
TRUST
between both
parties

If you complete this service cycle successfully, the *next* time you ask *"What is important?"*, the same person will tend to open up and tell you more. Why? Based upon their experience, they now have a reason to *trust* you. This is the foundation of long-term customer loyalty and success.

The assure quadrant is especially important. Done with enthusiasm and candor, *assure* leads right back to *explore,* with new possibilities and opportunities for both parties.

What would *you* do?

A new customer contacts you to place an urgent order. He is clearly in a hurry and wants immediate delivery. He knows the product catalog number and your price, but doesn't seem to fully understand what the product does, or how it actually works. *What would you do in this situation?*

During the installation of new equipment, an electrical surge damages one machine. The vendor charges you to replace the necessary components. You review the contract and see no clause about who is responsible in this situation. *Who should you talk with about this? What conversations would you have?*

Several new employees want to change their benefit package to include dental coverage. They are willing to give up other benefits in exchange. But your financial controller is hesitant, warning of the endless stream of modifications that might follow. *Should you accommodate the new staff or stick by the existing plan? Is there a middle ground? How would you find it?*

You overheard a conversation between your customer and her boss. They were complaining about how another company never listens to, nor implements, their suggestions. *What would you do to ensure they don't say this about you? Would you contact the other company to share what you have learned?*

Your top salesperson is frustrated. She closes deals easily, but Operations and Shipping are always late with delivery. *What would you do to help the company improve and help her close more sales?*

"You don't have to figure this out entirely on your own. Call a trusted colleague and talk it out."

UP Your Service! action steps

Make a list of everything you'd like to know about your customers. Make another list of everything you'd like your customers to know about you and your organization. Compile both lists into an attractive *New Customer Familiarization Kit.*

Go shopping for a new car. How many ways can it be customized for you? How many options do you have for payment and delivery? Shop for a new computer. How many choices do you have in price, features and configuration? Now think about a customer coming to *you* for service. How many choices and options do you provide? How quickly can you increase this number?

Post your delivery statistics where all staff can see them. Show trends as well as absolute numbers. Highlight areas in need of immediate improvement. (Want to improve your deliveries right away? Post the statistics where your customers can see them, too!)

Invite a cross-section of your customers to a special focus group meeting. Show them the four-stage service cycle of Explore, Agree, Deliver and Assure. Then share the staircase of service standards from Criminal and Basic, all the way UP to *Unbelievable!*

Using this scale of service standards, ask customers to rate your organization in each quadrant of the service cycle.

Ask what steps you could take to move higher up the stairs.

Finally, seek their input to prioritize which steps you should take first.

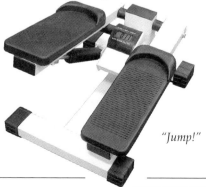

"Jump!"

8

Understanding
Perception Points

*Customers are constantly assessing, appraising
and evaluating the quality of your service.*

*During every interaction and throughout each
stage of the service cycle, customers form
impressions and opinions about you.*

*You can influence – and improve – these opinions
by focusing on the **perception points**
your customers experience every day.*

*Perception points are real. They are the
crucial moments when people see, hear, touch, taste,
smell – experience – you and your organization.*

*Each moment of customer contact, whether
before, during or after a sale or service,
will affect what people say and
believe about you.*

"PERCEPTION IS REALITY."
MARSHALL THURBER, CREATOR OF 'MONEY AND YOU'

Perception points are all around

The things people notice, appreciate and prefer are found in every aspect of your business. So are the elements they dislike, don't want and disfavor. Each of these key points of contact can shape your customers' perception.

Jan Carlzon, former President of **Scandinavian Airlines**, turned his company around with a campaign and a book called *Moments of Truth*. Carlzon claimed that *any* moment in which a person can form an opinion about you is an essential perception point, a moment of truth. He challenged the airline to master these moments and they achieved superior service.

Here's what you can do to manage and master *your* moments:

Study your products

Evaluate all your products' perception points: price, size, weight, variety, color, speed, strength, performance, level of innovation, design, materials, quality of manufacturing, built-in features, upgradability, reliability, durability, capacity, ease of operation, ease of maintenance, level of guarantee, eventual resale value and availability of technical assistance and spare parts.

Look at your people

Take a close look at your staff's dress code, personal grooming, eye contact, smile, posture and body language, tone of voice, choice of words, product knowledge, communication skills, punctuality, flexibility, confidence and motivation level.

Examine your place

Carefully inspect your physical location. Check maintenance and housekeeping, hours of operation, size of service area, quality of signage, access for differently-abled people.

Your website is an important place for doing business. Is yours fast to load, easy to navigate, attractive, up-to-date and secure?

Customers also receive service on the telephone. Are yours quickly answered? Do you have enough lines and staff? Is your automated system convenient and user-friendly? Do you have music or an attractive recording for customers waiting on hold? Is your telephone system ready to respond 24 hours a day?

Check out your packaging

Examine your packaging: its attractiveness, materials, design, instructions, ease of repackaging, recycling, waterproofing, weatherproofing and shockproofing.

Review your advertising and promotions

Is your advertising innovative, engaging and attractive? Does it project an appropriate image? Are your promotions well-thought out and effective? Do they reward the right customers for doing the right things?

Inspect your policies and procedures

Are your policies and procedures sensible, understandable and designed for ease of customer use? Do you make it simple to follow the rules? Do your customers feel welcomed, tolerated, or punished by your policies and procedures?

Evaluate your processes

Is your way of doing business smooth and speedy for your staff and the customers you serve? Are your processes fast or slow, simple or confusing, one-touch and one-stop or complex and difficult to decipher?

Want to *'Polish Your Perception Points'*? See Chapter 12.

Tune in to your senses

Perception points can be visual

Points you can **see** include grooming, lighting, housekeeping, color, size and design. These are the shine on your floor, the display of your goods, the pressing of your uniforms, the colors in your website and the typographical errors in your brochure.

Versace showrooms are masterful theaters of visual perception. The lights, colors, displays, flooring, ceiling and apparel of the sales staff are all chosen to produce an elegant visual effect.

Perception points can be auditory

Points you can **hear** include tone of voice, words in a script, background noise and music. These are your radio advertisements, on-hold telephone recordings, music in the elevators and public address announcements.

Tower Records makes shopping for music a pleasure. A world-class stereo system plays music in the shopping area. Carpets soak up any background noise. The telephone system is adjusted to eliminate intrusive ringing. Individual listening posts make it easy for customers to sample and select their personal favorites.

Perception points can be kinesthetic

Points you can **touch** and **feel** include weight, pressure and texture. These are the comfort of your chairs, the height of your counters, the temperature of your lobby and the calm firmness of your handshake.

United Airlines installed special seats with massage rollers built right in. **Virgin Airlines** went one step further on certain long distance flights – they put a *massage therapist* on-board!

Perception points can be gustatory

Points you can **taste** include products you sell and the food and drinks you serve. These are the variety of fine cheeses, the lingering bouquet of the wine and the freshness of your biscuits.

Visit **Stew Leonard's** grocery store. A big part of the experience is tasting! Nibble the cheese, dunk the donuts, lick the ice cream and sample the strawberries. Everything is arranged to help you *taste* the good things in life.

Starbucks has built an empire by expanding the tastes of coffee. Using beans and brains from around the world, now you can have your cup blended, iced, whipped, stirred, extra-strength, decaffeinated and even combined with juice. One item on the menu features decaffeinated coffee with low-fat milk and artificial sweetener. The drink is called *Why Bother?!*

Perception points can be olfactory

Points you can **smell** include scents, gases and aromas. This is the sweat on your brow, the disinfectant in the washroom or the freshly-cut flowers you put on the counter every day.

"Mmm! This service even smells good!"

Famous Amos builds outlets and positions ovens so the aroma of freshly-baked cookies wafts sweetly into the surrounding air. They leverage this perception point with a large banner behind the counter announcing *"Free Smells!"* Customers laugh at the banner, enjoy the aroma, and then they *buy* the cookies.

Perception points in the service cycle

Each stage of the service cycle is loaded with perception points. Here are a few of the most familiar examples:

Explore

What first impression does your company produce?

How quickly can customers get help and find needed information?

Are your staff competent, friendly and efficient?

Agree

How easily can customers place their orders?

Can orders be customized without difficulty?

Are your contracts user-friendly, without any confusing jargon?

Perception points are located *throughout* the service cycle.

1. Explore

2. Agree

3. Deliver

4. Assure

Assure

Is technical help readily available?

Do your guarantees work smoothly?

Is your satisfaction survey easy to complete?

Do you follow up with ideas and suggestions?

Deliver

Are products nicely packaged and well-produced?

Do deliveries arrive on time?

Are invoices and orders tracked correctly?

Are customers kept informed of special situations?

Focus on all four quadrants to successfully *UP Your Service!* Customers form opinions *throughout* the service cycle.

Perception points on an airline

- Is it easy to locate the flight schedule, fare schedule and seating arrangements for your itinerary?

- Can you easily compare routings and see the impact on your schedule and budget?

- Does the airline offer a package with hotel accommodation and car rental included?

- Is check-in fast and easy? Does the flight take off on-time?

- How is the food, the movie, the attitude of the cabin crew?

- Is the flight full or empty? Did you get an upgrade? Is there a screaming baby in the seat just behind you?

- Does the flight arrive on time? Are your bags on-board the flight? Are they quickly presented at the airport?

- Are frequent flier miles posted quickly and accurately to your account?

Perception points at a website

• Is the URL easy to read and remember?

• Does the website load quickly with your browser? If you turn off the graphics, does the website still make sense?

• Are the menus and hyperlinks easy to understand and navigate?

• Is there a site map or resident search engine to help you find exactly what you need?

• Does the website feature interactive multimedia? Does it have a privacy policy? Does it offer a money-back guarantee?

• If you order a product from the site, does the system send you an immediate confirmation of your order? Is another e-mail sent when your order is shipped? Is your credit card charged accurately?

• If you need help, do you get an e-mail reply right away? Can you click and be connected to a live service provider?

Perception points with a courier service

- Does the courier provide packaging free of charge?

- Do they offer customized computer software to help you enter and track your shipments?

- Do they have a 24-hour telephone system and website for scheduling pick-ups and ordering more supplies?

- Are the rates competitive? Do they offer special discounts for volume usage or large shipments?

- Are their drivers alert, on-time and well-attired?

- Do they pick-up and deliver on holidays and weekends, or only on weekdays during normal office hours?

- If you have a problem with a shipment, do they respond quickly and gracefully? Will they rebate shipping charges for packages inadvertently delayed?

- Are the invoices accurate and timely? Do they thank you for your business?

Perception points from the *pediatric dentist's* point of view

Let's face it, not many children *enjoy* going to the dentist. And some dentists don't make it easy for the kids!

Here's what may be on the dentist's mind:

- Is the **sign** for my clinic impressive? How much did it cost?

- Is the **door** to my clinic durable? Will it last a long time?

- Did the children mess up the **waiting area** again? Have they torn any more pages out of the books?

- Is the **nurse** back yet from her lunch?

- Will the patients be here on time, or will I have to **wait**?

- We need a **high counter** to keep the paperwork in order and safely away from patients, and especially away from the hands of little kids.

- Is **this kid** going to be a problem today? Last time she cried half the time and almost bit my finger!

It doesn't have to be this way!

At **Orchard Dental Centre**, the whole office is designed to set children and parents at ease. There's a special room with children's books and toys, an office full of friendly dentists, nurses and receptionists, a pantry with drinks and snacks, and even children's nursery rhymes to make the visit fun!

Perception points from the *young patient's* point of view

It's true! Most kids do *not* enjoy going to the dentist.

Here's what may be on their minds:

- Why is the **sign** so high? I wonder what it says?

- Why is the **door** so heavy? When will I be big enough to open it by myself?

- Is the **waiting area** fun? Are there any new toys, books or puzzles since last time I was here?

- Does the **nurse** remember my name? I wonder if she has any children as old as me?

- Why do we have to **wait** so long? Where is the dentist?

- What is Mommy doing at the **high counter**? Why is it up so high? I wonder what is going on up there?

- Is **this dentist** going to be friendly? Why does he cover his mouth when he asks me to open mine so w-i-d-e?

On my daughter's first visit to the dentist, he made an extra effort to set Brighten at ease and help her feel comfortable. She pressed the button to make the chair go up and down; she held the instruments and heard them hum and whirr. She tried on a dentist's mask, looked in the tooth-shaped mirror, asked lots of questions and told the dentist all about her day at school. And when he finally said *"Open wide"*, she did. She was glad to do it for her new *friend*, the dentist.

Perception points on a date

Perception points can enhance your personal life, too. The next time you go on a date, keep these points in mind:

- Is your invitation extended in person or over the telephone? By e-mail or personal letter? To the home or office? With a poem and flower attached?

- Where do you agree to meet? Is the location attractive?

- How are you dressed? Is it appropriate for the time of day and the activities you have chosen?

- Do you arrive on time? Perhaps a little early?

- Where will you dine? Which movie will you see? What else will you do together?

- Who will pay the bill? Should you pay for it in advance?

- How engaging is your conversation? Are you interested in your date, or talking all about yourself?

- Are you attentive to your date throughout your time together? Or do your portable phone and pager get first attention?

"On an enjoyable date, it's YOU that makes the difference!"

- Are you interested in going out again? Do you choose a time and date, or leave it at *"I'll call you sometime soon"*?

- Do you make sure your date arrives home safely?

- Do you call the next day to say *"Thank you"*? Do you send flowers or follow up with a pleasant note?

Identify *your* perception points

Around the service cycle

- What are the key perception points for prospects when they **explore** possibilities with you?

- What do people experience when they **agree** to place an order or negotiate terms with your organization?

- What do customers notice as you and your team **deliver** what you promised? What happens if there are problems during the delivery process?

- When delivery is complete, what do customers experience as you **assure** their satisfaction?

Using all your senses

- What do your customers **see** in and around your business?

- What do they **hear** from your staff and from your systems?

- What do your customers **touch** and **feel**?

- What do they **taste** and **smell** when doing business with you and your organization?

Finding the best and worst

- Of all your perception points, which would you rate amongst your *best*? Which give your customers the greatest feelings of fulfillment, contentment and satisfaction?

- Of all your perception points, which would you rate amongst your *worst*? Which cause your customers the most discomfort, displeasure or dissatisfaction?

What would *you* do?

Your staff's dress code has been gradually declining. Casual Friday has become a casual week. One hot day your guys removed their ties; some never wore them again. One young lady wore blue jeans to the office; now they all do. You'd like to improve dress standards without being autocratic. *How will you raise the subject? How will you raise the standard?*

One staff member has a nasal twang in her voice. Another has a strong regional accent. You want to provide voice coaching for both, but without offending either. *What is your plan of action?*

Your products look great in the showroom. But when they reach your customer, the packaging is all torn and dirty. You discover the low-cost couriers are at fault. They are rough with packages and their trucks are filthy. The drivers are dirty, too. You want better treatment and you don't want to pay a higher price. *How can you educate and motivate the courier to do a better job?*

You want to sell your house in a buyer's market. *What can you do to spruce it up and make it more attractive? If your intended buyer wants a real fixer-upper, what can you do to highlight the areas requiring his or her attention?*

"You can't hide from these questions. They need answers!"

It's a blind date. You have no idea whether your date will be dressed elegantly or casually for the evening. *What accessories could you wear or carry along? What can you put on, or take off, to match the situation?*

Perception points can be momentary while others are ongoing. Some points are direct, others virtual. *Which do you think are most important? Which deserve your first attention?*

UP Your Service! action steps

Sit quietly in your service area. Focus on everything that is red... then blue... then black... then green. With your visual senses heightened, look carefully for things that should be cleaned, painted, reworded, replaced or put away.

Wash your hands. Now thoroughly and slowly touch everything your customers will contact. What's rough, smooth and sticky? What feels good? What could feel better?

Cover your ears with your hands to block out sound. Listen to your breathing for a full minute. With your sense of hearing now heightened, remove your hands and take in the sound of machines, music, background noise and people talking. What sounds good? What grates on your ears? What can you do to improve the mix?

Examine your application forms, policy statements, instruction guides and other printed or digital information. Are they easy to read, easy to complete, easy to understand and user-friendly in every way? Find three specific areas to be improved. (My favorite complaint is order forms with tiny spaces to write your entire credit card number, expiration date and signature! What's yours?)

Pretend you are a customer. Follow the customer's experience from initial inquiry to final delivery. Write down *everything* your customer sees, hears and touches in your organization. Choose five points that can be improved right away.

Chapter 12 is packed with more ideas for polishing all your points. Take note!

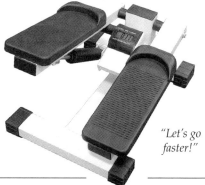

"Let's go faster!"

9

Understanding Value Dimensions

Question: What do customers really value?
Answer: It depends upon the customer!

What's important to one person may be of little concern to another.

Let's say a flight arriving from overseas is delayed
by several hours. What do the passengers want?

A mother with small children wants a place to change,
clean up the kids and get some nutritious food.

The business executive hunts for the nearest telephone
and the earliest onward connection.

An older couple on holiday want a nice hotel in which to
settle down and get some needed sleep.

And the young backpackers are eager to find a map
and begin their adventure in the city.

*Each of these customers **values** different **dimensions***
of a total service experience. And each of them is right!

To UP Your Service! you too must understand
what your customers want, need and value.

Some like it hard...

Many customers value the *hard* aspects of a service interaction. They evaluate a service experience based upon characteristics that can be quantified, measured and objectively assessed. Here are some examples:

- Access: *when are you available? where can I reach you?*

- Accessories: *which are available? which are included?*

- Accuracy: *did you do exactly as I requested?*

- Availability: *how long must I wait to get what I want?*

- Battery life: *how long do they last?*

- Certification: *are you industry certified? do you qualify?*

- Colors: *which are available? do they match what I requested?*

- Compatibility: *will this work with what I already own?*

- Cost of parts and labor: *what will it cost to keep this running?*

- Country of manufacture: *where was this actually made?*

- Cycle time: *how short? how fast? how much time?*

- Delivery: *how will you send it? when will it arrive?*

- Distribution chain: *is your retailer near my office?*

- Durability: *how long will this last before I have to replace it?*

- Efficiency: *what results do I get for my efforts?*

- Expiration date: *how much longer before this is obsolete?*

"Some folks value what they can touch and treasure."

- Features and functions: *what else can this do?*
- Guarantee: *what's covered, what's not, and for how long?*
- Location: *where are you located? are you close by?*
- Materials: *what is this constructed from? is it genuine?*
- Packaging: *do these come individually wrapped?*
- Performance: *how strong? how long? how high?*
- Portability: *pocket size? laptop? luggable? suitcase?*
- Power consumption: *how much energy is required?*
- Power source: *solar, oil, gas, hydro, wind, battery, human?*
- Price and discounts: *how much, for how many?*
- Procedures: *is it step-by-step or a tortuous maze?*
- Quantity: *how many, how large?*
- Rate of return: *how quickly will this pay back?*
- Recycling: *which components can be used again?*
- Reliability: *how dependable? what is the failure rate?*
- Remote control: *can I run this thing from over there?*
- Resale value: *how much will these be worth in a few years?*
- Running costs: *what does it really cost to own this?*
- Speed: *how fast to set up, run, take apart, maintain?*
- Temperature: *how hot? how cold? what range?*
- Trial period: *how long can I test it before I must decide?*
- Upgradability: *can I keep my investment up-to-date?*
- Variety: *how many different colors, flavors and sizes?*
- Weight: *how heavy, how light?*
- Zero defects: *is it close to 100% perfect, the very first time?*

Which *hard* value dimensions are important to *your* customers?

... and some like it softer

While *hard* characteristics are very important, many customers appreciate the more subjective and intangible elements of service. These *soft value dimensions* are more difficult to measure but are every bit as valid and important. Here are some examples:

- After-sales service: *do you follow up and follow through?*
- Ambiance: *is the environment nice to be in?*
- Animal rights: *were any harmed from making this product?*
- Appreciation: *are you really grateful for my business?*
- Approachability: *is it easy to talk with you?*
- Attentiveness: *am I truly uppermost in your mind?*
- Attractiveness of design: *does this look appealing?*
- Benefits: *will this help me get what I want?*
- Body language: *angry, friendly, tough, kind or eager?*
- Care: *are you genuinely concerned about my welfare?*
- Compassion: *are you empathetic? do you truly care?*
- Confidentiality: *will you protect my privacy?*
- Collaboration: *can you work smoothly with others?*
- Control: *do I feel in charge of the situation?*
- Courtesy: *are you tactful, appropriate and polite?*
- Craftsmanship: *is this made with skill, elegance and flair?*
- Creativity: *is it distinctive, original, unique?*
- Education: *will you teach me how it's done?*
- Endorsements: *who else agrees this is good service?*
- Entertainment: *is it fun or fascinating to be here?*
- Extra mile: *does your team go beyond the call of duty?*

- Fashion: *is it slick, is it now, is it hot and trendy?*
- Flexibility: *will you bend a little, or a lot, to make it work?*
- Freshness: *is it new, clean, innovative, crisp?*
- Friendliness: *are you welcoming, engaging and kind?*
- Generosity: *will you gladly give me a little bit more?*
- Greetings: *do you warmly initiate our interaction?*
- Grooming: *are you clean and attractive, well-dressed?*
- Helpfulness: *do you do all you can to make things work?*
- Honesty: *will you tell me the truth, protect me from harm?*
- Housekeeping: *is it clean here? is everything in good order?*
- Image: *what do people think about the company?*
- Initiative: *are you proactive and eager to take new action?*
- Listening: *do you really hear what I am saying?*
- Patience: *are you in a hurry, or will you take the time?*
- Peace and quiet: *can I rest here calmly for a moment?*
- Personal attention: *are you completely focused on ME?*
- Positive attitude: *are you upbeat and enthusiastic?*
- Progress reports: *do you keep me informed and up-to-date?*
- Safety: *do I feel secure here?*
- Support: *will you be there when I need you?*
- User-friendliness: *is this easy to understand?*

"Sometimes freshness counts!"

Which *soft* value dimensions do *your* customers cherish most?

Same *service*, many different values

Let's say you run a popular restaurant in the city. What do your customers want?

A **business executive** might want fast service, good food and a wide selection of current magazines.

A **romantic couple** could prefer slower service and a quiet candlelit table in the corner.

The **backpacker**? He's looking for low prices and big portions.

A **family with small children** wants a high chair and crayons, flexibility with the menu, and a *very* friendly waiter or waitress.

Same *product*, many different values

A pair of children's shoes: what are the value dimensions?

A **child** will look and say: *"Do I like the color? Is the design fun to wear? Are they comfortable?"*

A **parent** might ask: *"Do they fit well? Are they sturdy? How long will they last? How much do they cost?"*

A **sibling** could wonder: *"When will I get shoes like that? Will I get new ones, or will those be handed down to me?"*

And the family **dog** may well be thinking: *"I wonder if those new shoes taste good?"*

Common value dimensions

Many value dimensions are quite familiar. Customers look for them again and again in a wide range of **services** and **physical products**. For example:

Staff attitude: Is the salesperson pushy or patient? Will the telephone installation team clean up my home or office when they are done? Are the support technicians user-friendly people or aloof and arrogant nerds?

Reliability: Is the bus on time? Is my flight booked properly? Will the groceries I ordered on the Internet be delivered accurately? Does this product work as advertised? Was the television repaired correctly? Will you call me back as you promised?

Speed: Does the website load quickly? Can they deliver my books overnight? How soon will the repair service arrive? How fast does the new computer run? How long does it take for the virus scan software to download and check all my files?

Physical appearance: Is the hotel lobby neat? Are the rooms attractive? Are there fresh flowers on the counter? Is the mechanic's uniform clean or filthy? Does this product come in a container? Is the giftwrapping appropriate for the season?

Value for money: Is the price reasonable? Are there any extra or hidden charges? What is covered or excluded in the warranty? Do you provide anything extra for repeat customers or very large orders?

Flexibility: Can I make a change to the menu tonight? Can you deliver to my home after normal office hours? Do you accept payment in foreign currency? May I exchange this product for one that better suits my needs?

Personal attention: Do you remember my name? Do you know my needs? Can you recall what you said to me last time?

Want to add more *value*? Be sure you know *which* value to add!

In some markets, customers focus intently on getting a better deal, bargaining for a bigger discount and asking, even arguing, for a lower price.

The culture of price cutting can get so strong that some vendors talk enthusiastically about how little something costs, or how much you will save by doing business with them.

With a customer like me, that can be a big mistake.

Sure, I like getting a good deal, but I value *careful listening, customer education* and *personal follow-up* even more.

The vendor who promotes only *"Lowest Prices!"* has already lost my interest. I will gladly pay a bit more to do business with someone who:

- takes the time to truly understand my needs,
- helps me learn new skills and key distinctions, and
- stays in touch after the sale to assure my satisfaction.

Let's say you sell cars. Which is most important: speed, price, image, safety, personal attention, special features, service contract, gas mileage or interior and exterior size? *It depends entirely upon the customer!*

Key learning point:

In a world where *adding value* is a vital ingredient of business success, be sure to find out what *value* your customers really want!

Don't assume all customers are alike. Take the time to quiz, question and query. You will learn a lot.

Your customers will be glad you did. And so will you.

The ultimate value dimension

The ultimate in *UP Your Service!* is giving each customer what they want, exactly when and how they want it. This special level of one-to-one service matches every customer value dimension and features these seven characteristics:

1. You treat each customer as a unique individual, not as a member of some demographic or psychographic group.

2. Your service becomes *more personalized* over time. Each interaction is increasingly valuable for the customer. (Keeping the customer is more valuable for you, too!)

3. You build a learning relationship with each customer, discovering what they prefer in the present and delivering it in the future.

   On vacation at the **Ritz Carlton Hotel** in Bali, a waiter saw me reading the *Wall Street Journal* in the coffee shop. From that day onwards, it was automatically delivered to my room every morning. That's *UP Your Service!*

4. You help customers get to know you and work with you better. They become more efficient customers, understanding how to use your systems and your services to their advantage.

5. Your dialog with each customer is ongoing and deepening in nature. You observe their usage patterns and make adjustments or recommendations accordingly.

6. You ask for, and act upon, customer feedback. You show the customer how their recommendations have changed and improved the business. This builds loyalty both ways.

7. If the customer needs something you do not provide, you recommend someone who can provide that service. Customer loyalty still accrues to you as a valued and trusted service provider.

Different *values* all around the cycle

Value dimensions appear throughout the service cycle. Different customers can value different things. For example:

Explore

Speed: How fast can I get the information and pricelist?

Innovation: I appreciate your creativity and new ideas.

Endorsements: Who else is using this?

Reliability: Is the data on your website up-to-date?

Agree

Flexibility: Can we modify the terms and conditions?

Patience: Will your sales team give us the time we need?

Price: Can you give me a special discount?

Proactivity: What are your contingency plans?

Customers can seek *different* value dimensions in each quadrant.

Assure

Accessibility: Is your support available 24 hours?

User-friendliness: Is it easy for me to download help from the website?

Personal attention: Does your system remember who I am and exactly what I need?

Deliver

Accuracy: Did you deliver all the items I ordered?

Staff attitude: Are your people friendly, helpful and a pleasure to work with?

Cleanliness: Is your workshop clean? Is your delivery team well-dressed?

Your customers' wants, needs, priorities and expectations may be different from one customer to another. The only way to find out is to check with them regularly. *Ask!*

What do *your* customers value most?

Select your most important customers. Prioritize their top four value dimensions in each stage of the service cycle below.

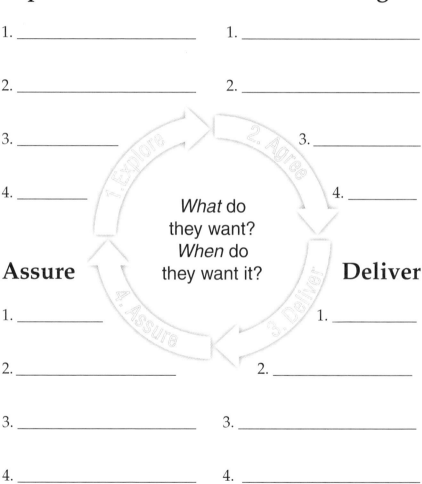

Explore

1. _____

2. _____

3. _____

4. _____

Agree

1. _____

2. _____

3. _____

4. _____

What do they want? *When* do they want it?

Assure

1. _____

2. _____

3. _____

4. _____

Deliver

1. _____

2. _____

3. _____

4. _____

Give your customers exactly what they want. Segment your customers by the service dimensions *they* value. Then focus your service improvement efforts to effectively *UP Your Service!*

What would *you* do?

Your company wants to 'segment the customer database' for an upcoming marketing campaign. Suggestions include segmentation based on geography, volume, size of company and length of customer relationship. You propose segmentation based upon customer value dimensions. Everyone looks to you for more details. *How will you explain this approach?*

Your new CEO is on a rampage to reduce paperwork. Reports are generated every month and nobody bothers to read them. It's been going on like this for years. You are asked to identify the few things that really count and are worth counting. *What are the most important value dimensions for your customers? How can they be measured? What are the key dimensions for your internal service staff? How will you track them?*

You run a successful website selling camping goods and hiking equipment. Your site is packed with customer-friendly information and plenty of good ideas. Now you want to increase the frequency and duration of customer visits to the site. You have $100,000 to spend. What new features will bring your customers back to the site again and again? Real-time weather forecasts? Interactive chat with experts? Extreme equipment reviews? A travel agency service? Streaming video of exotic trails and campsites?

"Which way do you want to take this?"

Which value dimensions will you select? How will you link these investments to boosting equipment sales?

UP Your Service! action steps

What do your customers value most? Make a list of what you *think* customers value most in the *Explore, Agree, Deliver* and *Assure* stages of your service. Pose the same questions to your colleagues in Marketing, Sales, Operations and Customer Service. Then ask your customers and compare the results. Where did you hit the bulls-eye? Where did you miss the target?

What is most important to your staff? Is it the pay, intellectual challenge, working environment, good colleagues, new learning, career development, management relations or other benefits? Have your staff list ten elements of value and rank them in order of importance. Align your actions to retain the best staff.

Think about your family. What do you value most in your relationships with your spouse, children, siblings and parents? What do they value most in their relationships with you? This week, do one more thing for each person that matches *their* values. If you like the result, do it again, and again...

Who values what you value? Take note of the advertisements and stores that appeal to you most strongly. What value dimensions are being offered? Which hold no appeal? Prioritize the dimensions that *you* value.

Select two customers. Think of three ways you can add *more value* to the relationship you have with them now.

Ask these customers to add more ideas and then prioritize the list.

Work on implementation, starting with your customers' first choice.

"You can do it!"

10

How to Get *Close* to Your Customers

Customers are a funny breed.

*They come and go, run away, stick around,
complain and compliment, and talk about you to others.*

*If you want to understand how they truly think and feel,
you need to **get close** and **stay close** long enough
to uncover their ideas, opinions and desires.*

*But how do you accomplish that with such
a diverse and unpredictable group?*

There is no single way.

*Rather, this chapter presents a suite of successful tactics
you can deploy to help you reach your goal.*

Understanding *means to stand under,
to fully comprehend the foundations
of a person or an organization.*

*To stand under your customers,
let's take a closer look.*

Do you really know your customers?

Customers have many different interests, issues and concerns.

How well do you understand…

- their business: *the dynamics of what they do, how they work, how they measure their success?*

- their industry: *the history, current changes and major issues of the day. What trends are rising, fading, or lurking over the horizon?*

- their customers: *who are they? Where are they? How many customers do they have? How is their customer base changing? Does your customer's customer have rising expectations?*

- their allies: *who are they collaborating with, and for what purpose? What's been working? What's not, and for how long?*

- their history: *their past glories, trials and tribulations, heroes, milestones and achievements.*

- their future: *what plans, directions and investments?*

- their technology: *what is installed and foundational? What is current, changing? What possibilities are they considering now?*

- their competition: *who are they? How many are out there? Who has market share? In what directions are they growing?*

- their internal politics: *who are their people? What are their preferences? Who holds the positions of power?*

- their procedures: *when and how do they get things done? Do they set goals, budgets and specific targets?*

- their hopes and aspirations: *what are they seeking? What do they want? What are their cherished dreams?*

- their concerns and fears: *what are they afraid of? What are the uncertainties, the downside risks, the dangers?*

- their opinion of you: *what do your customers think about you, your people and your organization? Do they see you as a valued ally or a necessary evil? Are they interested in working with you more closely or finding a replacement?*

Harvey Mackay, Chairman of **Mackay Envelope** and author of *Swim With the Sharks Without Being Eaten Alive* is a champion for knowing his customers well and serving them uniquely.

He uses a *66 Question Customer Profile* to learn everything about the customer from education, interests and lifestyle, to attitudes towards their company and career.

Mackay uses this information to fine-tune the service he provides and the relationships he develops over time.

How many questions do *you* ask about *your* customers? Do you know them well enough to stand apart from your competition? Do you understand what *they* want when you commit to *UP Your Service?*

Conduct surveys

Whether in print, in person or over the phone, nothing beats asking your customers exactly what they want and how they want it. Your survey can check current customer *perceptions* and track changes in *expectations*, too.

You can find out if customers are satisfied, if they plan to do business with you again and if they would recommend you to their friends or colleagues. If the answer to any of these questions is *"No"*, you can find out why and work to fix the problems. Want to know where you are really weak? Survey all the customers you've lost!

Surveys can be done either casually *("By the way, can I ask you a question?")* or more formally *("Hi, I'm conducting a survey. May I have a few minutes of your time?")*.

Surveys can be done by outside professionals or by your own staff and management team.

Surveys can be done continuously. **Singapore Airlines** surveys every fifth passenger on every fifth flight, every day, all year.

Surveys can include customer benefits or incentives. **Le Meridien Hotel's** customer questionnaire is called *Moment of Truth*. The form reads: *"For every questionnaire filled out, Le Meridien will donate $1.00 to a school for children with special needs. Thank you."*

Surveys can link to staff recognition. **United Airlines** asks customers to identify superior performers in their surveys and then rewards the staff with points, promotions and praise.

Set up a customer hotline

Some customers will tell you what they think, but want to do so anonymously. That's fine! What's important is that you get the feedback.

Set up a special hotline for customers only. Be sure your hotline staff are well trained in empathetic listening and practical problem solving.

Or you can use a voice recording system to capture customer comments. Promise to get in touch right away if the customer leaves a name and telephone number. (Try this *inside* your organization, too! Set up a hotline to receive comments and suggestions from your staff and then get ready to *listen!*)

Don't worry about receiving a few strange messages from insomniacs, former staff or raging nuts. Sort through the rubble to find useful and practical gems. If a customer has a genuine complaint, take action to fix the problem. If the caller makes a useful suggestion, put it to work right away.

And make sure your hotline is truly *hot*. I recently called a company's advertised hotline number. The recording said to call back during normal office hours, or leave a message at the tone. I waited to leave a message, and then heard another recording announcing that the voice mailbox was full!

Customer hotlines don't have to be by telephone only. You can provide a rapid response e-mail address or dedicate a specific customer service area. The point is not which way you do it – it's that you have a way!

"Our customer service staff are on-call to answer your questions 24 hours a day."

Visit your customer's site

Go to your customer's home or place of business. See with your own eyes what works and what doesn't, what gets used and what gets left behind, what is easy and convenient, what is unpleasant, troublesome and problematic. Then, make changes in your company to add more value and make things even better for your customers.

Include operational and customer service staff in your visiting team, not just the folks from sales and business development.

Prepare your questions in advance: What works for your customer? What is frustrating? What suggestions do they have for improvement? What else do they want to tell you?

Dear Valued Customer,

Thank you for your business. We appreciate your trust in allowing us to serve you.

As part of our ongoing efforts to serve you *even better*, we would like to visit you, at your office, for one hour.

The purpose of this on-site customer visit is to help us learn from you, first hand, how you actually use our products and services. As a result, our staff can make specific and immediate changes to benefit you more.

You deserve the very best from us and we are committed to providing it to you.

Please contact my office at your convenience by phone, fax or e-mail to arrange for this personal visit. Our staff will bring along a useful gift to thank you for your help and cooperation.

We look forward to hearing from you, and the pleasure of meeting with you soon.

Invite your customers to visit you

Bring customers *in* to see what, where and how you do what you do so well. Extend a sincere invitation and welcome them to your office, factory, workshop, warehouse, call center, service center, distribution center or other work-related locations.

By bringing customers *into* the organization, you bring down perceived walls and increase mutual trust. The resulting dialog can be priceless for building customer rapport.

You can roll out the red carpet, or just invite them for a practical tour. Make it a special event or a simple meeting over lunch. Get new staff and old hands working together to give your customer a useful education and make them feel genuinely welcome.

Greetings!

Every year we invite a few valued customers to our office for lunch and an afternoon tour of the factory.

We find these informal get-togethers very useful in helping us understand our customers better, and in helping you – our customer – learn a bit more about us.

Customers who have visited in the past say they appreciate the chance to see first-hand how we do what we do for you. This is also a great opportunity to ask any questions you may have and help us improve our service to you further.

Will you join us? Let me know what date is best for you and your colleagues and we will make all the arrangements.

Here at the office, this event is always a highlight of the year. Staff from many departments join together to prepare an interesting and enjoyable session.

I look forward to hearing from you and meeting you soon.

www.RonKaufman.com

Hire a mystery shopper

Professional mystery shoppers have a well-developed eye for detail that can help you see yourself in a new and revealing light. They can report to you on what works well and what falls short, where your perception points are strong and where you need to pay more attention. They can tell you where your staff provide great service, and where it's difficult to be delighted.

You can save money and increase your own awareness by serving as a mystery shopper at someone else's organization and then having them do the same for you.

Have someone you trust mingle with your customers and strike up conversations to find out what they do and do not like about your service.

Or do it yourself. Visit a branch office where you are not well known. Call in with questions while changing the tone of your voice. Send in a letter asking for a reply and see what kind of communication you receive. To know your customer, *be* your customer.

Todd Lapidus, founder of the **Customer Contact Corporation**, calls his mystery shopping a 'service chain evaluation'. Every step of the customer's experience is evaluated to see if it adds or subtracts service value.

You can be a service sleuth, too. Which value dimensions do your customers desire? Where do you increase those values? Where do you take them away?

Shop your competition

Become a customer with the best competitors in your industry.

If you work at a bank, open new accounts across the street. If you work at an airline, fly another carrier once a month. If you sell products on the Internet, become a vigorous shopper at all the other sites.

When you become a customer of your competitors, you can easily discover what is weak, unique or strong about their products, sales and service.

Try all your competitors' products and services and compare them to your own. Where you are doing better, expand your service advantage. Where you are doing worse, work hard to close the service gap.

You can also visit or shop your competition in discrete groups and meet afterwards to compare your experiences.

Imagine twelve staff from **Harrods** in London spending a week-end shopping spree at **Macy's** in New York. Over breakfast and during the plane ride home, the staff compare notes and share their insights.

What is Macy's doing well? How can we do even better? Where are we already ahead? How can we extend our lead?

What new ideas did you pick up? And, by the way, what bargains did you buy? I'll show you mine if you show me yours.

What a great way to learn something new!

Study complaints...

Every message from a customer brings value to your door-step. Compliments point out what to reinforce and continue. Complaints highlight areas for improvement.

Complaints can help you see where your products or services are below par. They can highlight staff who need more training or identify weak links in your systems and procedures. They can alert you to what your competitors are doing and give you an early indication of rising customer expectations.

Unsolicited complaints come in angry letters, upset telephone calls and face-to-face confrontations. Welcome them all. Beneath the rough exterior lies a tremendously valuable gift.

Solicited complaints come from asking customers what turns them off, what they do not like and why they might consider leaving you for another service provider.

Watch for trends. A decrease is a sign of progress. Increases deserve red-flag attention. A brand new complaint is something useful, an early warning signal worth observing.

"Today's customer wants more than just yesterday's performance."

...and compliments

You can get more than smiles and warm feelings from a careful study of customer compliments.

Which part of your operation is yielding the most praise? Ask the staff what they think they are doing right. Then have them help you fine-tune and polish other areas of the company that are not getting the same positive customer response.

If your waiters are getting rave reviews, have them work with the bellhops or telephone receptionists. If it's your Automotive department that earns the applause, ask them to spend some time with the staff in Garden Supplies.

If you invest heavily to improve an area and get no increase in compliments, you may have chosen the wrong customer value dimension. By contrast, if you make a small improvement and praise comes pouring in, consider investing even more.

If customers repeatedly admire a particular aspect of your service, you might see if they are willing to pay a bit more for it. After all, *UP Your Service!* is also about increasing your profits.

"Follow the pathway of praise to make your service even better!"

Focusing with focus groups

Focus groups require planning and expertise but they can be a gold-mine of valuable ideas, insights and suggestions.

Bring together a group of selected customers for a sincere, open-ended conversation. Set them at ease and get them talking about what they either like, don't like or wish they could get from your business.

If they could change one aspect of your service, what would it be? If they could wave a wand and make one requirement go away, what would disappear? If they had to choose between more of X or less of Z, which would they select and why?

Be clear in advance which questions you want the group to answer. Do you want comments on your current service, or advance feedback about your future plans?

Use presentations and storyboards to communicate key ideas. Engage a good facilitator to ensure everyone's voice is heard and the conversation stays on track.

Throughout the session, don't defend, justify or argue with the participants. Just ask more probing questions and take good notes. You'll gain a lot more value by listening than by speaking out to explain your current position.

Thank your customers with a sincere note and a valuable gift to demonstrate your appreciation. Let them know how their input will be used to make your service even better.

After the sessions are over, summarize key points. Then strategize or re-evaluate your service improvement planning. Take what you have learned and put it into action!

Benchmark inside and out

Benchmarking means comparing yourself with the very best. This can be done with leaders inside your own industry and with *UP Your Service!* organizations in other industries as well.

How do they do what they do so well? What best practices have they adopted? How are they changing and preparing for the future to maintain their leadership positions?

Benchmarking can be done on a tactical, process-by-process basis, or can be engaged from an overall strategic perspective.

Southwest Airlines benchmarks winning **Formula One** pit-stops for speedy turnaround of aircraft on the ground. **Pizza Hut** benchmarks **Federal Express** for on-time package delivery. The **Shangri-La Hotel** studies **American Express** for highest quality customer service call-centers. **Ikea** examines the military for excellence in coordination and logistics.

What about you? What processes are essential for your success? Who is the best in your industry? Who is the best in the world?

Look in professional journals *outside* your industry to find stories on those who lead the field. Contact them directly to arrange a benchmarking visit. As you are not a direct competitor, they will be flattered and open to your request.

"Take a closer look. Copy the best. Do better than the rest."

Winners of the *Malcolm Baldridge Award for Quality* are required to share their experience with others. This keeps everyone learning and improving.

What would *you* do?

You want to survey customers who have left you for another supplier. But few are willing to complete your forms or entertain your call. They are suspicious, thinking you only want to sell to them. Why did they leave? Where did they go? What do they think you need to change? *How would you explain the true purpose of your survey and engage their full participation?*

Your industry association is planning a benchmarking tour overseas. You are on the committee to organize the visits. Your colleagues suggest visiting companies like your own and see no purpose in visiting companies outside your industry. *What would you say to them? How can you help them see the value in benchmarking leading companies in other industries?*

While mystery shopping at a competitor's website, you see some information that is not completely accurate. The specifications are slightly off and the compatibility and upgrade charts are partially incorrect. *What would you do about it?*

E-mail queries, complaints and questions are increasing. But those who communicate by e-mail appear to be your least profitable customers. They tend to be younger and have smaller accounts than your more mature and established clients. They also expect fast replies and very detailed information. *What will you do in this situation? How much resource would you allocate to responding? Why?*

You are looking at complaints to get new ideas for improvement. Your managers don't like it. They don't like complaints. *How do you reassure them and gain their support?*

"That's a very good question!"

UP Your Service! action steps

Buy the same product or service from three different vendors. Ask questions, make exchanges and seek more information. Compare everything about the process. Who was easiest to work with? Who was most convenient? Which vendor was fastest, most flexible, most reliable? Which vendor (if any) followed up to check your satisfaction or ask for future orders? What can you learn from this exercise? How can you apply it in your organization?

When was the last time you:

- commissioned or personally conducted a survey,

- took calls on a customer hotline, or listened in on live calls while someone else responded,

- visited your customer at his or her place of business,

- invited customers to meet with you at your office,

- engaged a mystery shopper and read their entire report,

- became a legitimate customer of your best competitor,

- read a month's worth of complaints and compliments,

- ran a focus group, or observed one in process,

- did benchmarking inside and outside your industry,

- circulated the results of your efforts for everyone to see?

Are you doing enough to stay in close touch with your customers? What could you do more of? When should you get started?

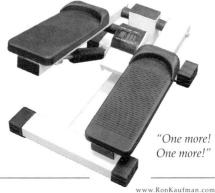

"One more! One more!"

11

Craft Your Service Vision

A strong vision is fundamental.
It gives people a sense of purpose, value and meaning.

A strong vision is inspiring.
It arouses feelings of ambition, enthusiasm and commitment.

A strong vision gives direction.
It provides an unmistakable idea of what is sought, and what is not.

Organizations often have written statements declaring their
commitment to excellent, superior and even world-class service.

While their intention is good, many of these statements fall flat.
They are not distinctive, motivating or clear.
Some sound like they were written by a conservative committee.

What does excellent mean? What does superior look like? How
would a team member know when world-class service is achieved?

Your service vision *should be uniquely and powerfully yours.*
Customers should hear it and say,"Yes! That is who you are".
Staff should read it and say, "Yes! That is who we want to be".

Sounds good? Want one? This chapter will show you examples that
work and provide guidelines to help you craft a vision of your own.

Call it what you will!

You can call your words a vision, mission, purpose, manifesto, strategy, objective or statement of service intent. You can have core values, guiding principles, a quest, a creed or even a code of conduct. Some call them marching orders. Others have company commitments. **The Motley Fool** has *rules for fools.*

It doesn't really matter what you **call** it. What matters is that you've **got** it!

What turns your customers *on?*

The first step is to identify which value dimensions really matter to your customers. Are these clearly reflected in your service statements?

Superlatives like *great, unsurpassed* and *legendary* may sound nice, but they don't give your staff a clear idea of what kind of service your customer wants.

By contrast, notice how **Avis Rent-a-Car** begins their mission statement:

"To ensure a stress-free rental experience..."

Avis knows that *stress* turns their customers OFF. Elimination of that stress becomes an anchor for the company mission.

The mission statement of **Adia Personnel Services** reads:

"Adia will be known as the easiest personnel services company to do business with. We are committed to removing barriers between us and our customers..."

Adia knows that *ease of use* is the customer's highest priority. And the mission statement makes that crystal clear.

What turns your people *on?*

Your next step is to write a statement using words and phrases that direct, align and motivate your staff.

- Don't settle for something flaccid like "We are committed to customer satisfaction". Stake out a bolder claim: **General Motors** strives to achieve *"Industry leadership through customer enthusiasm"*. **American Express** wants nothing less than *"To become the world's most respected service brand"*.

- Create a vision easily understood at all levels. **Marriott Hotel** says, *"Our commitment is that every guest leaves satisfied"*. That's pretty straightforward.

- Make your statement easy to put into action. The mission at **Tandy Corporation (Radio Shack)** is *"To demystify technology for the mass market."* It goes on to say, *"Our people are different because we get excited about helping people understand technology…We are about people helping people."* If you work at Radio Shack, you know exactly what's expected.

- Easy to understand doesn't mean easy to accomplish. One of the most productive mission statements in the world was presented by **John F. Kennedy** when he challenged **NASA** and the nation *"to put a man on the moon and bring him back safely by the end of the decade."* He said, *"We choose to do these things, not because they are easy, but because they are hard."*

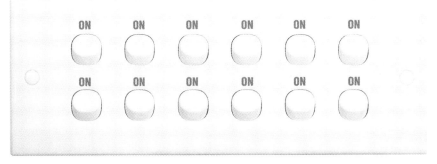

"Get your people powered up and switched ON, headed in the same direction."

The Raffles Hotel mission statement

Raffles Hotel is recognized worldwide as an icon of elegance and character. The famous hotel is impeccable, unique and pleasantly eccentric.

Shortly after the hotel's multi-million dollar renovation, I worked with the management team to write a mission statement worthy of this remarkable legend. The statement consists of just twelve words, each carefully chosen and charged with meaning:

> *Raffles is Singapore's*
> *grand historic hotel,*
> *delighting patrons with*
> *many memorable experiences*

Let me show you why each word was selected and how the final mission statement works effectively for the hotel today.

Raffles: Sir Stamford Raffles established The Lion City as a British Colony in 1819. His name is revered and respected.

is Singapore's: This small nation is intensely proud of the hotel. Its clean, classic facade and elegant turbaned doormen project the nation's image worldwide.

grand historic hotel: This is an elite class of hotel. Only a small handful of properties on Earth can claim membership in this exclusive category.

delighting: Raffles Hotel is not about satisfying needs or meeting expectations. They apply a much higher standard.

patrons: 'Customers' would not be enough. Almost *everyone* is seen and respected as a present or future patron of the hotel. This includes residential guests, customers at any of its seventeen food and beverage outlets, tourists, employees, suppliers, travel agents and tourism bureaus, journalists, shareholders in **Raffles International** and every citizen of Singapore who feels pride when they see the gleaming white exterior or hear the name 'Raffles Hotel'.

many memorable experiences: People do not come to Raffles for ordinary experiences. Hotel patrons want fabulous photographs, memorable dining, extraordinary accommodation, exceptional interactions with staff and unique souvenirs from the giftshop. My wife and I were *married* at Raffles Hotel. It was elegant. It was fun. It was *memorable.*

With the mission statement written, every department created a set of supporting *service values*. Then two customized training programs were developed for all employees:

The first, *Grand Historic Hotel*, teaches the staff key facts they can share with patrons: the origin of the 'Singapore Sling', the live tiger hiding under the Billiard Room, the grand tradition of New Year's Balls, visits by Charlie Chaplin, Rudyard Kipling and W. Somerset Maugham.

The second, *Many Memorable Experiences*, helps staff find new ways to create memorable levels of delight. Gardeners teach guests the names of tropical flowers. Doormen stand proudly for photographs with tourists. Valets explain who stayed where: Ava Gardner, James A. Michener, Michael Jackson, and now *you!*

"Raffles Hotel is home to many unique sights and sensations. Enjoy your visit soon!"

Your vision might be a moving target

Your service vision must keep pace with change. This means revisiting and redrafting your statements from time to time.

For years, **Motorola** aligned its worldwide team with this essential statement:

OUR FUNDAMENTAL OBJECTIVE
(Everyone's Overriding Responsibility)
Total Customer Satisfaction

Behind this unifying banner, Motorola launched their famous *Six Sigma* drive towards zero defects, a *10X* initiative for cycle time reduction and many other projects, programs and campaigns. They were so successful, they won the *Malcolm Baldridge Award for Quality* in 1988, the very first year it was awarded.

But times change. Motorola became too confident in its statistical approach, temporarily lost touch with important customers' needs and directions, and began to lose market share.

Motorola *now* understands that customer satisfaction may be just a momentary assessment, a mere snapshot in the evolving world of competition and customer expectations.

What Motorola really wants to achieve is long-term *customer loyalty*, identified by these three characteristics:

- a very high level of *current* customer satisfaction,
- a commitment to *future* purchases from Motorola, and
- a willingness to *recommend* Motorola enthusiastically to others.

This new vision for Motorola has a name and a metric. It's called *Top Box Quality* and signifies the company's commitment to continuous service improvement until every customer checks the 'Top Box' on Motorola's service and satisfaction surveys.

Keep these points in mind

- There is no right or wrong *length* for your service vision. **General Mills** takes three pages and 512 words to get their point across. **General Electric** uses just three words: *Boundaryless – Speed – Stretch.*

- Involve others when drafting and revising your service vision. You might ask the management committee to write a first draft and send it to others for response. Or you could have everyone submit ideas and blend them well together.

  Perhaps you'll run a contest, or hire a consultant, or have a flash of inspiration in the shower. There are many ways to reach the top. All of them can work.

- Keep your service vision out in front. Put it on the wall with signage, posters and illustrations. Put it in the mail with your newsletters and correspondence. Print it on your letterhead, business cards, T-shirts, caps, cartons and delivery trucks. Put it in the wallet of every employee. Pin it on your chest. Record it on your voicemail. Store it on your screensaver. Bring it up on the computer every morning.

  There are a hundred ways to keep the vision clearly in front of your team. How many are *you* using now? Which *new* ways can you apply?

Who is your service vision for?

Your service vision must speak clearly to a variety of audiences.

Your employees: The words you choose must educate, motivate and inspire your staff. These are the people who will bring your service vision to life.

Your customers: Your statement should appeal to those you serve. It should tell them what style of service and level of commitment to expect.

Your suppliers: These essential business partners must understand your service vision. Their service to you directly impacts what you can provide to others.

Your shareholders: Ownership in a company is not just about rates of return and profits. Use service statements to engage shareholders in an emotional, as well as a financial, investment.

Your community: The larger context for all our enterprises and endeavors.

Your competitors: Use your service vision to differentiate yourself from others in the industry. Let people know *why* and *how* you are unique.

Make your vision a challenge to all

'Meeting expectations' and 'complying with specifications' won't turn your people on. You need a bolder language to drive them strongly forward.

There is a practical reason why your service vision should reach higher. Research in schools reveals one consistent determinant of exceptional student achievement: the expectations of the *teacher*. When told that certain students were of exceptionally high intelligence, the teacher naturally expected higher performance from them. And although their IQ was, in fact, similar to all the others, those students excelled.

You are the superintendent of your team and the principal of your future. What kind of teachers and students do you want?

The National Library Board in Singapore has a powerful service mission: *"To expand the learning capacity of the nation so as to enhance national competitiveness and to promote a gracious society."* That's big. That's bold. That's *inspiring!*

Use this worksheet

What are the key value dimensions of interest and importance to your customers? (see Chapter 9):

What motivates your staff? Which service goals turn your people *ON?*

What is your current service vision statement? Underline any words that should be reconsidered or revised.

Write your new service vision here

"I don't score by skating to where the puck is now.
I skate to where the puck is going to be."
Wayne Gretzky

What would *you* do?

You have been selected to lead the process of recrafting your company's service vision. *How will you approach this project? Who will you ask to work with you? Where will you look for input, examples and ideas?* (Hint: search for 'Mission Statements' in the books section at **barnesandnoble.com**)

An e-commerce business has asked for your advice. They want to project a consistent service image on their interactive website, in their outgoing e-mails and through their conversations with customers on the phone. *What key suggestions would you give them?*

Your young daughter asks you why you work so hard. You explain that you love her, love the family and also enjoy serving colleagues and customers at your work. She asks what's so special about the service you provide? *How do you reply?*

At church, your young son discovers the weekly gathering is called a 'service'. He asks if there is a link between service in the business world and the service you attend on Sundays. *What is your reply?*

Mother Teresa: *"Where God is, there is love, and where there is love, there is always service."*

"Yes, you! Speak UP for superior service!"

Shirley Chisolm: *"Service is the rent we pay for our space upon the Earth."*

Albert Schweitzer: *"I don't know what your destiny will be, but this I know: the only ones amongst you who will be truly happy are those who have sought and found a way to serve."*

Now it's your turn:

Up Your Service! action steps

Visit three locations with service you admire. *Ask the managers to tell you their service vision statements.*

Visit the Ritz Carlton Hotels in New York. Ask any staff member, "What's your service mission?" Don't be surprised when they elegantly recite: *"We are ladies and gentlemen, serving ladies and gentlemen."* They have been well trained to know it, and do it.

Quick! What are the exact words in *your* service vision? If it's too long to remember, too vague to keep in mind, or if it simply doesn't exist, *launch a campaign now to craft or redraft this vital guiding statement.*

Where **is your service vision?** Can you see it on the wall, find it in a file or pull it from a card inside your purse or wallet? If it's out of sight, it's probably out of mind! You need *top of mind* awareness here, so keep these words in sight.

At the **Service Quality Centre**, a specialized service vision is emblazoned in the restrooms! An attractive sign requests: *"Please leave this place cleaner than you found it. Thank you."* That's a good example of person-to-person service!

Now look carefully at your current service statements. Which words or phrases turn you on? Which do you find vague or boring? Is the overall tone appropriate, current and inspiring? Or are you working with a hand-me-down from a bureaucratic committee that was retired long ago?

Don't get me wrong: timeless statements still ring true. *It's the dull and dated versions that must go!*

"Climb higher."

12

Polish Your Perception Points

A wedding day approaches.

*The blushing bride is at her finest: her hair,
make-up, dress and flowers are all in perfect place.
The nervous groom is equally well-attired.*

*The wedding hall has been prepared to host this celebration.
Every shining window sparkles in the light.
Each tall candle is new and softly glowing.*

*The music is uplifting. The flower sprays are radiant and full.
The wedding feast is a banquet of delights.*

*All this effort and attention. And for what purpose?
A glorious wedding!
A day to cherish, a time to treasure, a moment to remember always.*

*Now shift gears: when your customers come or
call for service, how important is that moment?*

*How prepared are you for that special day, that remarkable time,
those moments your **customer** will remember?*

Polish your *people*

Everyone in your organization should know how to look and feel their best. Whether you are mechanics, masseurs or masterminds of manufacturing, standards for your apparel and presentation should apply.

Start with dress code and fashion. Clean, color co-ordinated, properly fitting uniforms and attire are essential.

Move on to personal grooming. Examine hair styles, fingernails, make-up and personal scents. Getting this right makes sense.

Check posture and body language. How you stand, sit and place your limbs sends a powerful message. Eye contact and gestures count, too. A circle from thumb and forefinger can mean '*A-OK!*' in the USA, but something very different elsewhere.

Evaluate presentation skills. Confidence in public speaking gives your team a big head start. Provide coaching in voice, tone, projection and the use of scripts. Master the art of visual aids.

At **Singapore Airlines** it takes *four months* to prepare a famous 'Singapore Girl' for flight. Forty percent of that time is dedicated to first aid, safety regulations and essential security procedures.

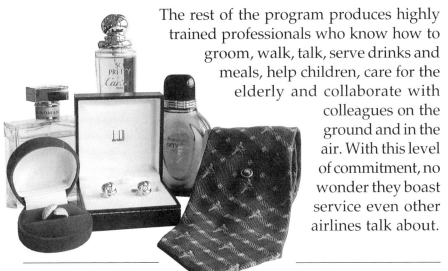

The rest of the program produces highly trained professionals who know how to groom, walk, talk, serve drinks and meals, help children, care for the elderly and collaborate with colleagues on the ground and in the air. With this level of commitment, no wonder they boast service even other airlines talk about.

Polish your *product*

Constantly upgrade and improve your products with research and development that works.

Examine your products' features and benefits. You can be the latest with the greatest, on the leading edge, or selling only tried and true solutions. Whatever position you choose, make your products effective, convenient and attractive.

Add on the bells and whistles! Put in something extra to make what you have stand out: better ingredients, automatic upgrades, batteries installed and included.

Mattel has extended the *Barbie* doll into every conceivable wardrobe, activity and occupation. Does it work for customers? You bet! How many girls do you think want just one Barbie?

Pricing can be used as a perception point to gain attention and customer action. Create special offers, volume discounts, package deals, holiday sales and once-in-a-lifetime bargains.

Häagen-Dazs knows you'll eat much more if the price goes down as the quarts, and calories, go up. Incentives to indulge are right on the menu: double dips, super sundaes, and every tenth cone you buy is *free!*

"Perception counts. Spread the word!"

But be careful here. Sometimes customers want to pay *more*. Your low price could produce a negative impression. Do you want a cheap diamond in your engagement ring? Are you looking for a bargain basement deal when investing in precious art? Would you cherish a **Rolex** watch that cost only a fraction of the normal price?

Make your product the very best from your *customer's* point of view.

Polish your packaging

What your service looks like on the outside tells customers a lot about what's waiting on the inside. This is what they see and think:

"Are your cartons poorly constructed? If so, the product inside could have quality problems, too. Is your delivery location a mess? I'll bet your customer service is also pretty messy."

Attractive packaging projects a positive image. Look at the fashion and cosmetic industries for indisputable proof!

The package alone can make a powerful statement. Consider **Tiffany's** light blue boxes, **Cartier's** rich red ribbons, **Intel's** sticker proclaiming: *'intel inside'*.

Appropriate packaging wins points with customers, too. Is yours durable, reusable, easily discarded, retained or recycled? Does your packaging convert to dual use? Is it well-designed to add more value, or is it just another container?

When **Disney Interactive** launched *The Lion King* on CD-ROM, parents bought the program as a holiday gift for their children. But on Christmas Day, many parents could not fathom the installation instructions and Disney's technical support lines were jammed all morning.

When *Pocahontas* was released, parents were encouraged to open the box *before* Christmas (without the children) and follow the instructions inside. Technical support was standing by for those who needed assistance. Once the software was loaded, parents used *another* attractive box enclosed *inside the original packaging* to rewrap the software gift. On Christmas morning, parents were proud of their achievement, children were elated with their gifts and Disney's technical staff were relieved.

Polish your *policies* and *procedures*

Ease of use is a necessary mantra for every *UP Your Service!* organization. Each process, policy and procedure should be completely *user-friendly*. Whatever your customers must understand, complete, fill-out or submit should be designed for maximum convenience.

When someone registers or buys for the very first time, are your steps intuitive and simple? Once the information is inside your system, must your customer ever repeat it? Is data passed from department to department? Are subsequent forms pre-filled?

Amazon.com has taken the lead by remembering who you are, where you live, how fast you want delivery and how you prefer to pay. Their patented *'one-click'* technology lets you buy a new book with literally just ONE CLICK!

What happens when a customer returns for a refund or replacement? Are your policies and procedures convenient? If they apply for credit or special terms, is the application a breeze?

If you have a discount club or membership plan, do customers need to carry the plastic card at all times? If they show up but left their cards at home, will you bend the rules in their favor?

Policies should accommodate unusual situations. Are your staff empowered to make good decisions? Or do customers have to wait while your staff run to check with the boss?

E-commerce is blasting a hole through traditional policies and procedures. The rules for bricks and mortar don't all apply in a clicks and mortar world. For example, if I buy on-line, can I return the goods to one of your physical stores? If not, why not? Whose ease of use are you protecting?

Rule Book

"This should be a user-friendly document. Is yours?"

Polish what can be *seen*

What your customers *see* makes a huge impact on their impressions of your service. *Look sharp!*

Is the lighting right? Are the colors appropriate? Is the condition of the wallpaper attractive? Are your furnishings clean and in good repair? Does the floor have stains and scratches?

At Hong Kong's Silicon Harbor, **Motorola** harnesses the visual sense to boost housekeeping around the plant. They take pictures of messy offices, overflowing filing cabinets and hallways cluttered with boxes. The photos are displayed on a bulletin board near the staff cafeteria with a frowning sticker attached. No names are mentioned, no locations provided. But within days the offending messes are removed. Then another photo is taken and posted on the board with a smiling sticker attached. Everyone gets the clear message.

Is your signage crystal clear, or do your customers wander at times in confusion? Is your website a joy to visit? Do the fonts, graphics, colors, video, audio and special effects support or distract from your message?

Are your manuals attractive? Are the instructions clear? Are warnings simple and straightforward? Are ingredients listed on the box? Are recommendations printed on the label?

Prudential stepped away from the crowd by printing insurance policies for customers in *plain language*. The benefits and regulations are exactly the same, but customer perceptions are much better.

Take a close look at your organization. With a bird's-eye view and penetrating stare, make an honest assessment. Are you a welcome sight for sore eyes or is your business a real eyesore?

Polish what can be *heard*

Listen up! What your customer *hears* in and around your organization should be in tune with the best of service.

Start with your receptionists, in person and on the phone. Do they enunciate well? Do they know what to say? Are their scripts up-to-date and well-written?

How do they sound? Is it music to your customers' ears? Do they purr like kittens, roar like lions or snap like alligators?

Check your voicemail. Is it clear as a bell and easy to navigate? Or do callers struggle to understand, or get stuck in an endless loop, forgotten in your voicemail dungeon?

When you put a caller on hold, what do they hear: silence, music, or your competitor's advertisement on the local radio station?

Check your doors. Do they squeak or swish? Are your floors carpeted to absorb the chatter? Is there a doorbell to announce arrivals? Does it honk or chime or sing a sweet serenade?

"Tune in to the sweet sounds of service."

When your delivery vehicles leave the plant, do they belch and rumble or is every car and truck well-tuned? Does your equipment grind from lack of attention or hum like well-oiled machines?

Is there background sound at your place of business? Do you control it or is it random? **The Rainbow Room** in New York understands the power of music to set the mood at mealtimes. They play celebration symphonies during business lunch, romantic classics at dinner and jazz late into the night.

Polish what can be *touched*

Make your service a positively touching experience. Review and improve every surface your customer holds or contacts.

When they want to sit, are there enough chairs? When they stand in line, does a carpet cushion their feet?

If they need to write, do you provide an attractive pen? When they open a package, does the cover get stuck, is the tape hard to remove, are components easy to assemble?

Is your atmosphere carefully managed? Do you control the temperature, adjust the humidity or create a breeze with fans for maximum customer comfort?

Another way you can touch your customers is with human contact. A fascinating experiment demonstrates the power:

Students leaving a university library were asked: *"How pleased are you with the service?"* The average rating was 2.7 out of a maximum 5.0.

The library staff were then asked to make very light and apparently incidental contact with the students: a mere instant of touch on the hand when giving back a library card, providing change at the cafe or handing a book to a student.

Satisfaction ratings shot up to 4.2 for the entire period of the experiment. Asked what was different, not one student could identify the 'touch' factor that had changed. Yet many said the library seemed more friendly and enjoyable than before.

The experiment was repeated at a busy restaurant during lunch. Waiters made the briefest of contact with patrons when holding a chair, taking a credit card or providing a new spoon or fork.

What happened? Tips jumped. Happy customers, happy waiters.

Polish what can be *smelled* and *tasted*

Have you got the sweet *smell* of service success?

Open the windows and let in a breeze or flavor the atmosphere with flowers, incense or perfume.

Top agents at **ERA Realty** use the power of this sensation when buyers are looking for a house. What better way to feel *at home* than to smell the aroma of fresh bread wafting from a kitchen? It doesn't matter that the bread was bought in a store and then simply warmed up again in the oven. The fragrance and memories are what closes the sale, not the location of the baking.

Do customers enjoy the *taste* of your service? **Singtel Mobile** places refreshing candies on the service counter. After all, mobile telephones mobilize the mouth. Captivating tastebuds can capture customers!

Gate Gourmet is a leading provider of catering innovation for the global airline industry. They worked closely with **Swissair** to create a *mis en place* dining experience in the First Class cabin. Meals are individually prepared in the kitchen on board (no longer just a galley) and brought to your seat with all the trimmings on the plate (no more service from the trolley).

*"A fine wine with your dinner, sir?
And how do you find the service tonight?"*
The passengers reply: *"First-class!"*

"Mmm..."

At infancy we identify our mother and father by their unique and memorable scents. When customers think about and identify you, is it a sweet memory they will recall?

How *fast* is this line moving?

Everyone waits in line. Few people enjoy it. Making a line move *quickly* is one way to keep your customers happy. Making your line *appear* to move quickly *also* makes customers happy.

Managing appearances means managing your customers' perceptions. It takes imagination. And then it takes action.

Here are some proven ways to do it:

- Be sure to have a *line*, not a mob scene or a crowd. An orderly progression towards the service area gives customers – and service providers – a sense of calm.

- Keep the line narrow. Single file lines move more quickly than two or three abreast.

- Arrange the line so those waiting can *see* the person currently being served. Watching another customer being served makes your place in line appear closer. When the actual service is out of sight, around the corner or down the stairs, *your* turn can seem many miles away.

- After each customer is served, use a light, arrow or pleasant chime to announce to everyone *'Next!'* This keeps the next person alert (saving time between customers) and gives everyone a regular assurance that the line really *is* moving.

- Put a time estimate on digital display. Let people know what to expect the minute they join the line.

- Provide information alongside the line to attract the attention of those who are waiting. Hang posters, provide

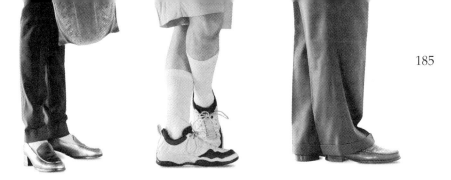

brochures, put reading material where they can reach it. When customers become involved, time flies faster.

- Play music in the waiting area. For a young crowd, choose upbeat and energetic tunes. For a more mature audience, choose instrumental or classical compositions.

- Put a television or video-screen in clear view for those in line. Choose an appropriate channel for your customer base: **CNBC** or the **BBC** for a business crowd, **Martha Stewart** for home lovers, **Mr. Bean** for everyone who could use a smile.

- Hang mirrors along the line. **Otis Elevator** discovered this years ago. When mirrors are placed near elevators in the lobby, people eagerly start checking their appearance. They get so involved, they hardly notice the time taken for the next elevator to arrive. You can use the same approach.

- Engage the remaining senses. Play music, display freshly cut flowers, offer something to drink or a selection of sweets. At **Aspen Mountain** ski area, boxes of facial tissues are provided alongside the lift lines. People are grateful to blow their noses, wipe their brows and *enjoy* a moment of rest.

- When the wait is truly long, send your staff to 'comb the line', interacting with customers in advance. You can answer questions, provide information and thank them for their patience.

So many ways to manage perceptions, just while waiting in line! *Any* customer perception point can be effectively polished to a positive *moment of truth.* Pick one now that needs your attention and put your imagination to work!

Put your best foot forward

You never get a second chance to make a first impression. So make your first ones count!

Give extra attention to your advertisements, front door, shop windows, website home page, marketing brochures, telephone greeting and initial contact.

When the **MGM Grand Hotel** opened in Las Vegas, they needed to hire thousands of new staff in a hurry. They didn't have time for extensive profiles, so the first round of screening was this: if you came down the hall and smiled at the staff, you were directed towards an interview right away. If you looked at the staff with confusion or concern, you filled out a form and were told, *"We'll call you if we need you."* Then you were directed politely to the door.

Even the tax collector has a perception point or two

The Tax Department sends you notice of an audit. That's bad. But the writing is user-friendly. That's good. The appointment is at a convenient time and location. That's good. But the auditor is running late. That's bad.

In the lobby is a magazine rack. That's good. But the magazines are two years old. That's bad.

The auditor is friendly. That's good. And the audit goes smoothly. That's good.

But you still owe more money. Too bad!

Do you feel the need for speed?

One popular value in today's business world is getting things done *fast*. This dimension can be polished to give customers the speed they need.

You can increase your counters, telephone lines, computer power, number of trucks and head count. You can give your staff the tools they need to handle many tasks on automatic.

You can ensure sufficient bandwidth to serve peak periods on your website. Every month, my newsletter, *The Best of Active Learning,* goes out to thousands of subscribers around the world. A surge of hits returns immediately to the website. We must have capacity to meet the demand! No sense driving traffic to the site if it leads to an unpleasant digital jam.

Leave a good impression when you go

Last impressions are lasting impressions. Be sure you wrap up every interaction so your customers look forward to seeing you again.

Summarize important points. Restate your promises and agreements. Say, *"Thank you"*, and show you mean it. Send a follow-up message or a handwritten note.

Comedian **Bob Hope** was famous for saying, *"Always leave them wanting more."* He did that by delighting his customers before he left the stage. You can do it, too.

What would *you* do?

A regular customer gives you a large plant to help spruce up the office. The plant looks great, but its flowers emit a strong and not-so-pleasant aroma. *What would you do with the plant? What would you say to the customer?*

Your customer has a piece of spinach stuck between her teeth. *Do you tell her about it? Should you? If so, how?*

Your new staff member has no fashion sense. He mixes plaids with paisley and summer shirts with boots. He's the boss's son. *How do you approach the subject? What should you do to help him?*

The office is a mess. Everyone agrees to come in during the weekend to do spring cleaning. But you want more than a general clean-up; you want a *substantial* boost in appearance. *What instructions would you give the team first thing in the morning? What planning would you do before the date? What benchmark would you propose? What special resources might you provide?*

You have a global market for your products. But in some countries your price must be significantly lower to compete. You can save costs with less expensive packaging, but you also want to maintain a strong brand image. Regarding the cost and quality of packaging, *how low should you go?*

"Make the decision. It's up to you."

You hire professionals to conduct a perception point audit. They find problems with your suppliers, which in turn affect your firm. *How would you raise this with your suppliers? What would you say to your customers? How would you involve your staff?*

UP Your Service! action steps

Control the background music. Get some new music from a selection of artists – classical, jazz, rock & roll, disco, new age, vocalists and blues. Play them one by one in the office. Ask staff what they enjoy hearing at different times of the day and in different departments. Ask your customers what *they* would like to hear. Take control of the tunes!

Go shopping with your team. Carefully notice the color, decor and lighting in a good jewelry store, bookstore, clothing store, hardware store and supermarket. *What works? What should be changed? What can you apply at your place?*

Put on white gloves. Gently stroke the surface of all the seats, tables, cabinets and paintings in your office. Still white?

Cookies, fruits, chips, nuts or candy? Coffee, tea, juice, soda, hot chocolate or sparkling flavored water over ice? *Which do your customers prefer? Which do you provide?*

The perfume industry spends millions every year promoting passion, possibilities and pleasure. Women and men spend millions more to choose the perfect fragrance. *How much do you spend to make your office or outlet smell nice?*

Pretend you are a brand new customer. You are from overseas and the local language is not your first language. Carefully review all the information, document-ation and instructions that come with your products or service.

What can be made easier to read, follow and under-stand? Change the words, the illustrations, or both?

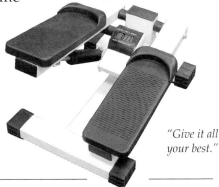

"Give it all your best."

13

Make Your Customers
Information Rich!

*Whether you are buying a car, building a house,
choosing a computer, planning a vacation,
having a medical check-up or filling out a wardrobe,
one powerful ingredient you definitely need
is useful, accurate **information**.*

*Some vendors provide only the most basic facts and figures:
price, specifications, availability and terms.
These vendors attract customers who want
fast delivery, low price and often a special deal.*

*Other vendors provide a wealth of information:
instructions, insights, ideas for use, examples, case studies,
descriptions, history and related background.*

*These vendors attract customers who appreciate the effort
it takes to gather and provide this **information**.*

*This kind of customer makes recommendations, helps others and
contributes new ideas. And, they are willing to pay more money.*

*Who would **you** rather buy from?
Which vendor would **you** rather be?*

What makes the difference? *Information!*

Two families fly into an exotic city for a long-awaited vacation. Each rents a car from a different car rental company.

The first family is given a spotless car with a full tank and a very nice smile from the attendant. They drive out of the airport parking lot...and promptly get lost.

At the other company, the family is given an identical car with a full tank and a very nice smile from the attendant.

They are also given a map of the area with key routes to major destinations clearly marked.

They receive a Tourist Guide, already translated into their native language. Local terms are included, with a pronunciation guide to help them with the most basic and useful phrases. The guide has an up-to-date calendar of things to do in the area and a complete listing of hotels, shopping centers, restaurants and tourist attractions.

As they drive, a pre-installed global positioning system shows them exactly where they are and guides them towards their chosen destinations. Later, when they are looking for a hotel, the system provides accurate directions along with current room rates and vacancy data. No sense driving to find a hotel that has no rooms for the night.

At the end of the trip, the first family takes home a frustrated feeling of never being quite settled, always asking for directions and occasionally getting lost.

The second family returns home with terrific memories of all the things they saw and did, impressed by the ease and convenience of their travels.

What makes the difference? *Information.*

Don't let *your* customers get lost. Make them *information rich.*

Overwhelmed and overloaded is *not* the same as *rich!*

Sheer volume of data, facts and figures does *not* guarantee success. Information is only valuable if it's *what* customers want, presented *when, where* and *how* they want to get it!

No sense having the latest information about weather on the ski slopes, unless you are thinking of skiing. Not useful to have the recipe for eggplant lasagna unless you are planning dinner. And it's foolish to overwhelm someone with in-depth maintenance instructions if they haven't yet made the decision to buy.

One credit card company scared customers by having too much information! When a card holder called for assistance, 'inbound caller identification' let service representatives know before answering who was waiting on the line. The representatives began by saying, *"Hello Mr. Kaufman. Thank you for calling again. How may I assist you this time?"* The card company thought it was great. Customers thought it was scary.

Your challenge to enrich others with information is two-fold:

First, you must gather appropriate data and genuinely useful insights. Mechanisms to do this can include your staff, automated tracking systems, customer feedback, consultants and so on.

Second, create convenient, effective ways to get the information directly to those who want it. Use 'push' technologies like instructions on the side of a box and outgoing e-mails to customers. Or use 'pull' techniques like a website full of FAQs, a fax-back or call-in system, or a catalog of drawings and data that sits on your customer's shelf.

"The right information in the right way to the right people at the right time. That's the key!"

Who should be information rich?

Your customers are all the people who will use, or have ever used, your products and services. They come to you to enrich, improve, protect or expand the quality of their lives. It's up to *you* to show them how!

Not-yet customers (usually called 'prospects') should get attractive information to help them understand who you are, what you have to offer, and how you can help them achieve their objectives. When they can gather useful information in an engaging and timely manner, prospects are likely to buy.

New customers need very specific information to help them get accustomed to your systems and get the most value from your service. When new customers understand how to work with you easily and effectively, they are most likely to continue.

Existing customers deserve customized information to obtain maximum benefit from their ongoing relationship with you. Customers who are well-informed will recognize the value you deliver. And customers who appreciate value are customers who keep coming back for more.

Everyone in the company should understand these objectives. In a very real sense, the entire organization is involved in the marketing and customer service process. **Steven Howard**, author of *Corporate Image Management*, says it this way: "*If it touches the customer, it's a marketing issue.*"

Who?

Wise words worth remembering and sharing with others.

Colleagues and employees in your department and other departments should definitely be kept well-informed. From shift to shift, office to office, or location to location, these are the *internal service partners* you rely upon to get things done.

A lousy service organization calcifies into 'silos', rigid internal bureaucracies where communication happens only at the top.

A great service organization promotes vigorous internal sharing of information: status reports on current projects, upcoming plans and promotions, and vital customer feedback. Marketing announces what's coming. Sales tells what's selling. Operations keeps everyone up-to-date. And Customer Service feeds back to the entire organization about what is pleasing the customer, and what is not.

Your business partners and allies will do a better job if they are well-informed about your current needs and future aspirations. *Suppliers* can help you most when they understand your priorities and future directions. *Dealers, agents* and *resellers* will be more effective in the market when they have the information they need to compete. And *joint venture partners* deserve your finest business insights. Together you must look ahead to invent a vibrant future.

Shareholders around the world insist on full disclosure. Investments now move with a single call, the stroke of a key or click of a trader's mouse. Withholding information in such a forceful field is not the way to win.

Your community wants to know what you are doing and how. *Educational organizations* in the community should also be informed of your current and emerging labor needs.

The media can be your ally with good public relations, or your nemesis with investigative reporting. Better to be proactive and keep them up-to-date. World news has shown time and again that trying to 'hide the truth' is an invitation to disaster.

What makes people information rich?

Provide your audiences with a wide range of useful content to keep them well-informed.

Your service vision is a good place to begin. Explain who you are and why you exist. What is your mission and your purpose? What values guide you? What principles are you committed to uphold? Where did these statements come from? What do they mean today?

Company history provides a connection to your past and a link to the future. Highlight the founding mothers and fathers, your early years, the milestones and the achievements.

Your products and services can be described in great detail. What do you offer? How does it work? What benefits and features do you provide? What strengths and capabilities do you promise? Are there any important areas of weakness?

How are your products designed, sourced, manufactured, installed, tested, regulated and delivered? Is maintenance required? If so, when and how is that accomplished? Is self-service an option?

What does it take to keep your products in optimum working condition? What return on investment can be expected?

Are your products compatible and interchangeable with others? Or do you use a proprietary system? What goes well with what you sell? What should be avoided?

What do you have in stock right now? How long will it take to deliver? What are the steps for making a purchase? What payment terms are allowed?

What makes your products and services different, better, more valuable or cost-effective than all the others in the market? *Why should I buy from you?*

Who are your customers? Where are they located? What are their issues, aspirations and problems? How do you help them obtain good value? Why have they chosen you over all of the others? What special relationships have you developed? What do other customers say about you? What references and testimonials can you provide?

Contact information is essential. Where are your locations? Are you open only during certain hours and days of the week? What are the telephone numbers, fax numbers, e-mail and website addresses? Who should I contact with which kinds of questions? How long will it take you to reply?

Your team members can be featured, too. Who works where? What are their skills, backgrounds and special interests? Provide selected information for external use and a wider range for internal networking, dialog and exchange.

Case studies can show how existing customers use your service to their advantage. Provide typical examples and unusual requests. Show how your services can be customized for special needs and situations.

Industry jargon can be explained for those unfamiliar with it. Become the provider people respect for clear explanations, education and understanding.

Facts and figures can be useful. Provide statistics, specifications and historical data to help customers understand trends and directions in your market.

When to make people information rich

Twenty four hours a day is the right time to provide clear and practical information. The expression "24 – 7 – 365" didn't exist in my grandfather's time. Today, it's considered the natural pace of business.

Anniversaries are excellent times to keep your customers informed. Birthdays are good if you are a cake maker, insurance salesperson or driver's licensing bureau. Weddings and anniversaries make sense if you are a florist or a jeweler. The anniversary of a customer's purchase or installation is a great time to provide information – especially if you offer annual maintenance contracts!

During selection, preparation and consumption of your products and services is the right time to provide useful information. When do you look at the nutritional information on cans and boxes of food? And how many times have you read the back and side panels on a box of cereal while you ate the same cereal for breakfast?

At **Stew Leonard's**, a large sign answers the question: *"When is the best time to shop?"* A colorful chart shows customer traffic volume in hourly increments throughout the day. Slow periods are marked, *"The best time to shop"* while very busy times are indicated, *"You'll see all your neighbors!"* Customers make their own decision on when to buy groceries. And because they are forewarned about busy times, there are very few complaints about shopping delays.

When?

Any time can be a good time to provide useful information. Some people want lots of it before they make a decision. Others seek input when negotiating the agreement. Most people appreciate being informed when something important is in process.

Explore

Prospects and interested parties seek a wide range of helpful information. You need to provide it. When someone says, *"Just looking"*, it means they want to know more before making a decision.

Agree

Closing the sale and making a deal means more than just terms and conditions. Present all the options for detailed discussion. Put your cards on the table. Build a reputation for fair and honest dealing.

Useful information is valuable *throughout* the service cycle

Assure

Keep customers informed after the delivery is over and they will remain your customers much longer.

Send updates, upgrades and consumer reports. Give them new ideas to get more value from their purchases.

Deliver

Information is crucial during this stage. Give them plenty of answers!

How is it going? Where is my order? When will your team deliver? I've got this installed, now how does it work? Which page of the manual applies?

The Internet and 24-hour channels like **CNN** have dramatically expanded our information expectations. People want to know and they want to know now! Can you answer their questions?

Where to provide rich information

You can find so many places. Here is a list to get you started:

- *Advertisements* in every possible medium, from television and T-shirts to Internet, radio, magazines, newspapers, brochures, posters, flyers, stickers and even double-decker buses.

- On your *packaging*, inside and out. **Celestial Seasonings** prints information and ideas on every surface of the box.

- On the *product* itself. Where do you need the instructions for an emergency flare or fire extinguisher? Right *on* the product.

- Your *website* is an obvious place to provide information including marketing material, FAQs, user's manuals, consumer reports, specification sheets, case studies, testimonials, databases, relevant articles, instructions, interactive bulletin boards, discussion groups and more.

- Your *contracts* can include more than just price and policy numbers. Add appendices to add value to the agreement.

- Use your *physical premises* to provide information. Cover the walls with educational posters. Open a library. Start a museum loaded with history. Install computers connected to your website. Put in counters for face-to-face questions, and telephones for instant access to timely information.

  - On your *delivery vehicles*. **U-Haul** puts attractive images of national landmarks on the side of their trucks. They also list the price of renting that vehicle and a phone number for making your reservation.

Where?

How to make people information rich

- Use words, symbols, music, quotes, quizzes and cartoons. **Apple Computer** uses color-coded cables to teach you where to plug in the wires: green goes to green, red goes to red. In just minutes your computer is up and running.

- Put the information in writing. Provide it on the telephone. Make it available in audio and video and through inter-active educational designs.

- Make your information *mandatory* by requiring a response before the customer can move forward. Software licenses require a 'click' before you can use the program. Many websites insist that *"You agree to the terms and conditions stated above"* before you can access the content.

- Or make your information *optional* (but always available) with context sensitive menus, options and help. Providing information that is *just enough* and *just in time* increases the comfort and confidence of your customers. You don't bombard them with unnecessary information, but you are right there with answers when they need it.

- Provide information *just in case* to assure people it's there if they need it. Every good hotel room has a map on the inside of the door showing *'You are here'* plus instructions for survival and the best escape routes in case of fire. You don't want to have to search for this information if the need arises, you just want to read it and *go!*

Why make people information rich?

Useful information can help people become more effective and fulfilled. Customers become more satisfied. Suppliers become more efficient. Colleagues better understand what needs to be done and how to work smoothly together.

At **Squaw Valley**, downhill skiers know what to expect as soon as they join the chairlift line. A digital map shows the waiting time at each of the lifts on the mountain. With this information skiers can make informed decisions about where to ski next. And waiting times are kept low across the mountain.

Greater information leads to greater involvement. **Dell Computer** changed the paradigm by giving customers access to detailed information about products, inventory and pricing. At their website you find all the facts about available hard drives, video-cards, modems, memory, screen sizes and much more. You can design a computer to match your needs. And once you have designed it, you are very likely to *buy* it.

Useful information anticipates questions and provides answers, building trust. **The Body Shop** offers extensive information about how products are made and tested. More data is on hand to help you choose products for your skin, hair and complexion. Customers trust the brand and return for more because they trust the product information.

Well-presented information increases comfort and participation. **The Motley Fool** hosts a wildly popular website offering thousands of pages of insights, opinions and statistics. But the primary offer under *Investing Basics* is called *Take 13 Steps to Foolish Investing*. New visitors are coached clearly on where to go, how to get started and how to continue their growth.

The more people know, the more they tell others. Successful multi-level marketing companies like **Amway** and **Mary Kay Cosmetics** are vibrant examples of information leading to more products, more customers and more sales. Their events and materials are packed with education, explanations, illustrations, case studies, laboratory reports and motivating personal stories – all of it, information.

Information helps people get more value and enjoyment from their purchases. My friend collects owl figurines. Hundreds are roosting in her office. And what does she seek now to increase her enjoyment? Books, videos and websites, all about owls!

Information encourages people to invest and acquire more of what they want. Every collector knows that information makes one piece more valuable than another. **Sotheby's**, **Christie's** and other fine houses have taken this to an artform of its own. The *provenance* of a piece tells the history of an item. It is the *story* that sets the prices high and stimulates the urge to acquire.

The more people know and understand, the more likely they are to contribute useful ideas and suggestions. The operating system **Linux** grew from an open approach to sharing and evolving information.

Purchases are often emotional decisions, backed up by rational facts. Buying a new **BMW** or **Jaguar** can be a satisfying experience. Data about the cars is convenient.

Sit in the driver's seat and gauges tell you the temperature inside and out, the level of fuel, the distance you have traveled, your coordinates on the global positioning system.

Good information. Nice to have. But is that why you bought the new car?

What would *you* do?

You are the marketing and public relations manager. One of your products has a minor flaw that poses no health or safety risk. Less than 2% of all your customers will be affected by the situation and most of them won't even notice! *What would you do in this situation?*

(**Intel** had a similar situation with an early version of the *Pentium* chip. They learned a lesson the hard way. *Will you?*)

Your company has a rather colorful past. One major product recall a decade ago, a couple of lawsuits recently settled out of court, and a scandal about your CEO's private life that got flushed through the press last year. You are the public information and investor relations officer. *How much information should you provide about these matters? Where will you make it available: in person, in print, on the telephone, on the Internet? What will you say to those who ask for more details, who want to know 'your side of the story'?*

The FAQ (Frequently Asked Questions) section of your website has taken on a life of its own. The volume of questions from customers has your support staff overwhelmed. You could (a) maintain full control and responsibility for the content of the site; (b) open this section of the site to greater customer participation, allowing users to contribute answers as well as ideas and questions; (c) spin off this section of the website entirely, opening the site to industry-wide participation with information on competitors products as well as your own. *What is your decision?*

"Yes? No? Which way to go?"

UP Your Service! action steps

Go to the Microsoft website. Ask any questions about the company, its services or products. Count how many pages of relevant information you receive. Now visit your own website. Ask similar questions. How much information is provided?

Dig into your company history. How long does it take to dig it out? Now put it in a form that someone else can easily locate and enjoy.

Run a *'What do you want to know?'* campaign with your customers. Compile a list of everything they say they'd like to know about your organization, products, people, services and more. Have them prioritize the items on the list. Then get to work giving them what they want, step by action step.

Information needs to flow inside the organization, too. Use attachments and cross-training to improve understanding between departments. Use web-based bulletin boards to promote awareness between physical locations.

Call all your competitors and ask five questions. Make notes of your experience and record all the information provided. Now call your own company and ask the same five questions. Where did you get the most information, and the best presentation? The next time you do this exercise, make sure the best of the best is yours.

Select articles of interest to your customers. Send them out with a simple note attached. Create a customer-focused newsletter or magazine. Send ideas, insights, examples and information. *Always stay in touch.*

"Keep going strong."

14

Cultivate Customer Contact

Can I have your attention?

This call's for you.

Did you get my e-mail?

I left a message on your machine.

There's a letter here addressed to you.

A package arrived this morning.

Did you see the latest update on your home page?

Whew! That's a lot of contact.
Sometimes it can be overwhelming.

In this context of busy daily lives, your
*contact with customers must be **appealing**.*

In person and in writing,
on the telephone or on the Web,
*make it **enjoyable** and **rewarding***
*for customers to hear from **you**.*

Cultivate contact *face-to-face*

Listen to the whole person. When engaging your customers face-to-face, don't just listen to their words. Discover the background of concerns behind the language spoken. What does this person care about, what does she want, what are her hopes and fears?

This *context* for the conversation is essential for building connection with those you wish to serve. What culture do they come from? What are their standards for appropriate behavior? How do they assess good from bad, safe from uncertain, precious from merely common? What evidence do they prefer to see when establishing or agreeing upon value?

Ask good questions to keep the conversation moving. 'Open' questions probe for greater understanding. *"What are your objectives? What do you hope to accomplish? What do you wish to avoid?"* 'Closed' questions move the conversation to another level of decision. *"Do you want that delivered now or next week? Are you familiar with the maintenance process? Do you have any other concerns or questions right now? Are you ready to place your first order?"*

Use your sensitivity to set others at ease. Find out what they want and provide it.

If your customer is anxious, be reassuring. If she's excited, be enthusiastic. When he's confused be clear, calm and patient. When she's committed, be equally certain.

This is not to say that you should blindly mimic your customer's mood or manner. But do what you can to set them at ease. Provide comfort to those around you.

"Kindness is love in motion."

Offering compliments is another fine way to cultivate customer contact. We conducted an experiment at a client's service center to fathom the power of praise. I instructed the counter staff to quietly praise each customer's attire when they came to the counter for service. Men were told, *"That's a nice tie you have on."* Women were complimented on their clothing, hair, earrings or necklace.

As the customers left they were asked for their opinions on the quality of customer service. Nothing had changed in the speed, products or systems, but the customers' ratings were higher.

Be generous to others in all your interactions. You really have nothing to lose. If someone is thirsty, offer a drink. If hungry, provide them with a snack. When someone is tired, give them a place to sit down. If they need to write, offer your pen. Does that person look confused? Offer directions. Do they want to know more? Provide the needed information.

Whenever I am in an airport or near a tourist attraction, I see people taking photographs of one another. Someone is always left out of the picture holding the camera. I offer a creative solution. I walk up and gesture towards the camera and towards the subject. Without fail they understand my meaning. They huddle together with enormous smiles while I play *photographer for the moment* in their vacation.

Take genuine interest in the cares of other people. Let it show when you meet them face-to-face.

Werner Erhard said it well: *"If you want to be popular, be interested. If you want to be lonely, be interesting."*

Cultivate contact with *body language*

In the field of *neurolinguistics*, there is a simple technique called *mirroring and matching*. The essential method is to copy (or mirror) the actions of someone else, or to mimic their actions in some way (matching). If you speak quickly, I will pick up the pace. If you take a slower approach, I will slow down to meet you. If you cross your arms, I may cross my legs. If you gesture with your hands, I may nod my head in agreement.

The purpose of this technique is not to do a parody of *monkey see monkey do*, but to establish a subconscious rapport between two parties. You can develop this feeling of comfortable contact with many different parts of your body:

- *Appropriate eye contact* is a universal way to show you are open to contact. While there are cultural considerations to keep in mind (some cultures are more direct than others, though no one appreciates staring), avoiding eye contact altogether is a sure way to kill the conversation.

- *Facial expressions* are important to get your welcoming message across. Smiling works. Curiosity can be effective. Scorn and anger are sure routes to shutdown.

- *Your posture* says a lot about where your attention is focused. Leaning forward slightly shows interest. Slouching back or leaning away are cues to disinterest and boredom.

- *The positioning of your arms and legs* shows your receptivity to ideas and other people. Crossing them both is an obvious way to close-out contact with others. Maintaining an open stance lets people know you are open to hearing their views.

- *Your gestures* are interpreted every time you speak, move and listen. Open palms and gracious moves welcome new conversation. Clenched fists, pointed fingers and punching into the air tell others to keep their distance.

I saw a remarkable example of body language in action at a conference with **Anthony Robbins** in Colorado. A leading instructor of *Neurolinguistic Programming* (NLP) was speaking to the group. One student offended the instructor. The instructor was incensed and stormed out of the room in a rage. Robbins moved to resolve the situation in a memorable and physical way.

Placing his large body between the instructor and the door, Robbins apologized sincerely. His face was open and his hands spread wide. As he spoke, he brought his body *down to a lower position* than the considerably shorter instructor. The instructor accepted this gesture of respect and stayed at the conference.

Cultivate contact on the *telephone*

Telephones amaze me. Pick one up and tap the keys. Almost instantly you are connected to another human being across town or across the world. In seconds, that inanimate piece of plastic supports a real-time, person-to-person interaction.

Make the telephone a powerful tool for connecting with your customers and delivering *UP Your Service!*

Make them happy that they called

Pay attention to your:

- *speed:* talk too fast and people struggle to understand you. Talk too slowly and people struggle to stay awake.

- *tone:* put energy in your voice and other people feel it. Drone on in a lifeless monotone and people feel that, too.

- *clarity:* articulate clearly and succinctly (enough said).

- *choice of words:* use customer-friendly language.

Say, *"Good morning. This is (your name) at (your company or department)"*, rather than an empty and anonymous *"Hello?"*

Say, *"I'll be glad to help you"*, rather than *"Let me see if someone can help you."*

"It's for you!"

Say, *"I'll call you on Monday at 9:00am"*, rather than *"I'll try to call you back."*

Say, *"Can you repeat that for me, please?"*, rather than *"What did you say?"*

Say, *"Can you hold on for just a moment, please"*, rather than *"You hold on, eh?"*

Make your transfers trouble-free

You can pass a call between colleagues *without* passing the buck. Follow these simple steps to get it right:

- express appreciation and explain the reason for the transfer,

- pass on information you've gathered on the caller's behalf,

- explain the transfer may take a moment.

What you actually say might sound like this:

"Thank you for calling and telling me what you need. The best person to help you with this is my colleague (fill in their name) in the (fill in the blank) department. I will transfer your call now and pass on this information so she can help you right away. This will take just a moment. Thank you for your patience. I will transfer your call now."

Be sure someone is on the other end when you make the transfer. Don't send your customer to a voicemail recording unless you let them know in advance.

If you are the person *receiving* a transferred call:

- address the caller by name,

- thank them for their patience,

- confirm the information you received, and

- ask further questions or explain what actions you will take.

"Hello (use your customer's name). This is (your name). My colleague, (his or her name), has explained your situation to me. May I ask you another question to be sure I fully understand? "

Leave a positive last impression

Say *"Goodbye"* with style:

- review the situation,

- promise appropriate action, including future contact,

- establish contingency plans,

- close with appreciation for the call.

"I understand the situation and what you want done. I will take care of it personally. If anything unexpected comes up, I will call you early next week. And thank you again for calling. Have a very nice day!"

Cultivate contact with *voicemail*

Ring. Ring. Click. *"You have reached the voicemail box for Extension 8146. After the tone, please leave a message."* Beep. *"I'm sorry this voice mailbox is full. Please call again."* Click.

Few innovations in modern life please, upset, delight and infuriate like *voicemail*. This tool can be used to your tremendous advantage, or it can destroy your reputation for service.

Record an outstanding outgoing announcement

Few people *prefer* getting your voicemail instead of reaching you live. You need to compensate with a well-crafted message.

- Use an upbeat tone of voice. Why should I leave a message for someone who sounds bored or angry?

- State clearly your name and your company or department. Who wants to leave a personal or detailed message for *'Extension 8146'*?

- Thank your caller for leaving a message. Many people are not thrilled about talking to machines. Let them know you appreciate the effort.

- Change your voicemail every week or every day. Tell callers where you are and when you will return. But only do this if you can sustain the habit. There's nothing worse than hearing *"Today is February the fourth..."* when it is actually March the third!

- Let callers know when to expect your reply. If you are on vacation for several days, tell them you will call them back next week. If you return calls several times a day, tell them you will get back in touch within 24 hours.

- Give callers an alternative to leaving a message. If their need is urgent, tell them how to reach another person right away. If they want to write to you by fax or e-mail, give them the necessary number and addressing information.

Leave an excellent voicemail message

When you leave a voicemail message for others, make yours stand out with clarity, effectiveness and style.

"Please leave a message."

- Use tone of voice to convey the meaning of your message. If you've got good news, sound energetic. If bad news is why you are calling, tell them with your tone. If the matter is crucial and needs attention now, let urgency crackle in your voice.

- Remember, you are making a recording that will be played back at a later time. What if the person you call is picking up messages from an airport or taxi? If you race through your message they may miss your meaning altogether. Speak slowly and clearly.

- State clearly who you are and the reason for your call. Who wants to get a message that says, *"Ron, this is Bob. Call me."*

- Suggest when and where they can call you back, or what actions can be taken. You can eliminate telephone tag by leaving clear instructions to move things forward one step.

- *Always* leave a telephone number clearly in your message. The person you call may be out of the office when they pick up your message. If you want to be extra sure, say your number in two different ways. *"Hello Robin. This is Ron calling you back about custom printing of my book for your staff. You can reach me today after two o'clock at four four one, two seven six zero. That's double-four one, twenty-seven, sixty."*

- If you want a fast reply, leave a message that sounds like this: *"Hi Ruth? It's Ron. You know that important project we've been working on? Well, I've got good news. Call me when you get a chance."* You'll get a call back right away!

Cultivate contact in *writing*

Writing is a powerful and enduring means of expression. From cave drawings and stone tablets to parchment and paper; in newspapers, books and magazines; on computer screens and personal digital assistants – the written word prevails.

Write person-to-person. Don't just send anonymous forms and boilerplate text that start out, *"Dear Sir/Madam".*

Every year I receive computerized invoices for insurance premiums due. Thousands of dollars in annual premiums, *and commissions,* but no one sends me a letter. It would not be hard for one company to *stand out* from the others. Just write!

Send cards on birthdays, anniversaries and graduations. Send congratulations whenever your customer succeeds.

Write articles of interest to your customers. Submit them to newspapers and industry publications. Then mail copies to your customers with a small note attached: *"I thought you might find this useful."* This builds your credibility and expertise. 'Author' and 'authority' share the same root: *to influence others.*

Attach personalized notes to your products. Put them inside the box, paperclipped to the report, or on top of the pillow if you run a hotel! I send color brochures and videotapes to clients all over the world. But they tell me the item that catches their eye is the personalized, handwritten note.

With word processing, laser printing, faxes, scanners and voice recognition software, the *handwritten letter* has become more unique. Use this to your advantage by picking up the pen and writing your customer or colleague a 'real letter'.

Remember the joy of a note from home tucked inside your lunchbox? Recall the good feelings from a handwritten note that accompanied chocolates or flowers? People remember the efforts you make. Let customers feel good remembering *you.*

Write compliments to encourage

When you get great service, write a great note to reward and recharge the service provider.

Acknowledge the high level of *quality* service you received. Tell them exactly what they did that stood out from all the others.

Describe the *impact* of their service. Detail how their positive treatment made your life, your day or your purchase much better.

Explain how the experience *exceeded* your expectations.

Make clear your intention to spread positive word of mouth and do more business with them in the future.

Compliments like these serve two functions. They make you feel good and inspire providers to continue with *UP Your Service!*

Write complaints that carry clout!

A good complaint letter can make the difference between suffering and getting service. When you have a problem, follow these steps:

State clearly who you are, what happened, when and where. Give a clear statement of the facts, without exaggeration, threat or venom.

Describe the damage done, frustration felt, or anxiety you experienced. If you lost time or money, state the amounts with evidence and a detailed accounting.

Explain exactly what you want done to resolve your situation. Express your concern for quick resolution, and by when you expect a reply. If you have a suggestion to help the company, now is the time to make it.

Close with thanks from a legitimate customer who has a problem and wants an *UP Your Service!* response.

Cultivate contact using *e-mail*

E-mail takes your message and zips it around the company or the world in an instant. But watch out! E-mail can be a double-edged sword. It cuts time, accelerating communication and improving customer service. It can also cut your career and credibility if managed poorly.

- Everything you write could be circulated, subpoenaed, copied and resurrected. *'For your eyes only'* is not a secure command in the digital world. Write only what you would accept others (perhaps *many* others) reading.

  The Russians have a saying: *"A word is not a bird."* Once a word is out, you cannot bring it back.

- Read and reply to your incoming e-mail *quickly*. Customers use e-mail instead of letters or fax because it is fast and convenient. They expect a fast and convenient reply.

- Copy relevant parts of the original message into your reply. Make it easy for others to recall what the dialog is all about!

- Create and use a signature file appended to the end of each message. Include your name, company, title and telephone number. Add a few more lines of copy if you wish, but keep it short. Four to six lines is the maximum.

- Create a reader-friendly 'subject' for every outgoing note. Some people receive hundreds of e-mails a day. Your subject heading can help your message get the attention it deserves. *'About the meeting'* is *not* a good example.

- Be thoughtful about whom you 'cc' in your outgoing mail. Including people without strong interest is a sure way to have your e-mails ignored in the future.

- When writing the message, spelling, punctuation and formatting do count. In some cultures *"r u coming 2 the mtg 2nite?"* is acceptable. With external customers it is not.

- Phrases like "&*#$%@" are not good form face-to-face. It's not a good idea to put them in writing, either.

- DON'T SHOUT! Using capital letters is considered *very loud* in digital communication. Use it only when you need to make an URGENT point.

- Use e-mail to stay in touch with your customers throughout the *UP Your Service!* cycle:

    explore: answer questions, provide detailed information, refer prospects to existing customers for testimonials.

    agree: dialog on terms and conditions, develop drafts and then document the agreement.

    deliver: send regular updates to keep your customer informed: orders received, confirmations, shipments.

    assure: follow-up with a message to confirm their satisfaction, and another to seek their suggestions.

- Steer clear of fancy fonts and characters unless you are sure your customer can read what you send. **Bold**, *italic* and <u>underlined</u> text can look like this □□□□to your reader!

- Avoid sending attachments unless your customer expects it. They take up space, require more time to view and can be problematic if you don't have the same software.

- Do not send unsolicited offers, proposals or invitations. These unexpected e-mails may be unwelcome and can backfire when customers start complaining. Instead, ask customers and prospects if they *want* to know more. Then build a service dialog that leverages their permission.

Cultivate contact at your *website*

The World Wide Web makes providing *UP Your Service!* easier than ever before. But customers can leave your site and visit your competitors' easily, too. The net result is this: customer expectations are rising. Your service efforts must fly even higher!

- Your website must be *fast.* The entire Internet universe is just a click away. Customers won't wait around.

- Information on your website must be *accurate* and *up-to-date.* Customers won't stand for an inventory listing that's obsolete, specifications out-of-date, pictures of products that no longer exist, or exchange rates that expired last year.

  The websites at **Fidelity Investments** and **Charles Schwab** feature stock quotes just 15 minutes behind the market. *Fifteen minutes.* Are you keeping your site current?

- *Frequently Asked Questions* can anchor customer service on your site. Every time you help a customer understand an issue, navigate a problem or choose between two options, take that knowledge and post it as an FAQ.

  - Make your website *navigation* easy to understand and follow. Provide clear *internal links* on every page. Offer a site map or *search engine* if your website is extensive.

"Turn your customers ON, on-line!"

  - If it is appropriate for your company and useful for customers, include *external links* to relevant resources.

.com

- Make e-mail an extension of your website with a strategy to 'push' *requested* information to your customers.

  Use *autoresponders* so customers can get data, articles or information sent to them conveniently by e-mail.

  Create an *opt-in newsletter* to keep your customers updated, aware and well-informed.

  Provide *automatic notification* so customers can be informed when new pages are added to your website or when new products and services are available.

- Encourage your customers to help themselves. Provide easy *downloads* and *upgrades* so they can get what they want, whenever they want it.

- Encourage your customers to help each other. Encourage a sense of community with bulletin boards, discussion groups and an interactive database of questions and responses. At the **Autodesk** website, customers help other customers answer thousands of questions each day.

- Customize and personalize your website experience to the highest possible (and profitable) degree. Capture voluntary information about your customers and then route towards what serves their interests. Remember what they viewed, asked about and purchased in the past, and automatically update their display.

- Integrate service at the website with service at your physical locations. Unless you are building a web-only business, customers should be able to shop, buy, ask questions, seek assistance, file reports, upgrade and return merchandise, or make payments at *either* your physical or virtual location. 'Bricks and mortar' are becoming 'clicks and mortar' in the business world of the future.

- Remember that a website cannot serve and satisfy every customer situation. Make it easy to connect to a 'real person' by e-mail or by telephone whenever the need arises.

What would *you* do?

Customer profanity is not unusual at your facility. It's part of the culture for this particular customer group. One of your staff is easily offended. The moment she hears a foul word, she hangs up the telephone or turns her back on the customer. *What would you do in this situation?*

Several of your key staff are telecommuting from home. This lowers costs and increases employee satisfaction. But two customers complained when they heard a baby crying in the background. *What are you going to do about it?*

Your customers want "24 – 7 – 365" support. You could set up call centers overseas to get round-the-clock coverage at a reasonable cost, but you are trying to move towards self-service customer support on the website. *Where would you invest? More call centers to keep customers happy now? A stronger website to build towards the future? Or divide your resources between both?*

Voicemail in your firm has created a blizzard of forwarded messages and broadcasts. A bad habit of shifting responsibility to others through forwarded voicemail is now appearing. *How will you keep the technology and reduce the negative behavior?*

The customer bulletin board is a smash success. Users post questions and answers, and help one another with problems. One competent contributor frequently mentions your competitors' products and services, pointing out the differences with yours. *What would you do about this? How would you manage this contributor's replies?*

*"Life is a contact sport.
What kind of contact is up to you!"*

UP Your Service! action steps

With your customer's permission, videotape face-to-face service interactions at your counters, showrooms and workshops. Do the same on audiotape with telephone service and support conversations. Use both sets of tapes in your in-house training programs. Ask employees to observe, compliment and constructively critique their own and their peers' performances.

Go on a voicemail safari. Call ten different companies after office hours. Listen carefully to their pre-recorded messages. Explore the menus. Try out all the options. Make a list of what works well and what doesn't. Now call your organization after office hours. How does your system measure up?

As you read newspapers and magazines this week, ask yourself, *"Who would be interested in this article?"*. Clip out the articles and mail them to your customers, colleagues and associates. Attach a short note to each article: *"Thought you might be interested to see this. Best regards!"*

Create or improve your e-mail signature file. Include your name, title, company name, mailing address, telephone, fax, e-mail address and website. Add a one-line message appropriate for your business, or an entertaining bit of personal wisdom. (For an archive of fun signature lines, see **www.coolsigs.com**)

Spend an evening surfing, gathering information and buying goods on the Internet. Shop for books, music, vitamins, vacation destinations or cars. Make a list of the website features you use and really admire. Check if your website offers them, too.

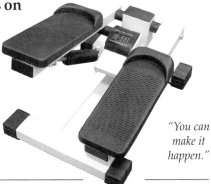

"You can make it happen."

CHAPTER

15

Bounce Back with
UP Your Service!
Recovery

*Things will go wrong.
It's an inevitable dimension of life on Earth.*

*When it happens, customer expectations tend to drop
while fear and anger often rise.*

*No wonder many service providers try to run away, hiding from
the damage, minimizing cost and shifting the blame to others.*

*But wait! When problems occur you can **bounce back**
and rebuild customer loyalty even higher than before!*

*With the right tools and understanding, you will regain customer
confidence and make your organization even stronger.*

*This chapter shows you how to get it right
…the second time around.*

*"Service recovery is turning a service failure into
an opportunity you wish you never had."*
MICHAEL HARGROVE

Problems can be *good* for you!

When things go wrong, customers will complain. That can be *good* for you and *constructive* for your organization. Customer complaints can:

- highlight areas where your systems require updating or improvement,

- identify where your procedures are a pain in the neck and need to be revised,

- reveal information that is lacking, erroneous or has simply gone out of date,

- identify staff who need more training or closer supervision,

- help monitor service levels and check consistency between shifts, departments and locations,

- get important news straight to the boss's desk (complaints have a way of getting noticed),

- educate everyone about what customers experience, expect and insist upon receiving, and

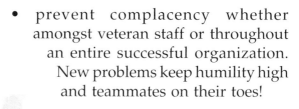

- prevent complacency whether amongst veteran staff or throughout an entire successful organization. New problems keep humility high and teammates on their toes!

"FAILURE IS SUCCESS,
IF WE LEARN FROM IT."
MALCOLM FORBES

"Some people cringe when they get
complaints but to me they're a gold mine
of improvement ideas and value."

On top of that, complaints also:

- help focus your attention, priorities and budget,

- work as a trigger for taking new action, catalyzing positive change,

- help raise staff morale as changes and improvements are made throughout the organization,

- keep you in touch with emerging trends and changing customer expectations,

- present new business opportunities for raising revenue, solving problems and increasing value to customers,

- provide competitive intelligence, letting you know what others in your industry are doing that you are not (yet),

- indicate which customers are willing to speak up. These people can be invited to participate in customer focus groups, beta-tests and on-site visits,

- give you case studies and needed content for your in-house training programs, and

- provide dynamic feedback for you to publish, with your replies and action steps, inside your company newsletter. **Singapore Airlines** reprints customer complaints and compliments inside the monthly staff newsletter, *Outlook.* Guess which section of the newsletter staff are sure to read each month?

Most of all, complaints give you an opportunity to reply, respond and win back customer loyalty. Most upset customers just walk away and complain about you to their friends and colleagues. (Negative word of mouth can be caustic.) The few who speak up are giving you another chance! Take it.

> *"When everything seems to be going against you,*
> *remember that the airplane takes off*
> *against the wind, not with it."*
> HENRY FORD

Make it *easy* for customers to complain

Complaints can be *good* for your business. So make it *easy* for your customers to give you the good (bad) news! Here are some proven ways to encourage fast and candid feedback:

- Set up a telephone hotline with 24-hour customer support. Encourage customers to call. List the telephone number on all your product packaging, instructions and sales material. Make sure staff who answer the calls have the mindset, toolset and authority to take action and set things right.

- Provide comment cards at key points of customer contact. Put the collection box in plain view. Print a statement on the cards expressing your genuine appreciation for customer feedback, promising a speedy reply.

- Post customer complaints and company responses in a public area. Be sure your responses show you have taken the complaint seriously, either with changes and action in the organization, or with a constructive and detailed reply.

- Welcome feedback on your website. Make it easy for customers and visitors to send you an e-mail message. And don't require them to fill out a detailed database before giving you a piece of their mind.

- Train your staff to solicit customer feedback at various points of contact. Asking, *"Is there anything we can do better for you the next time?"* accomplishes two important objectives. First, you gather valuable ideas. Second, you get the customer thinking about doing repeat business...*the next time.*

"ONE OF THE SUREST SIGNS OF A BAD OR DECLINING RELATIONSHIP WITH A CUSTOMER IS THE ABSENCE OF COMPLAINTS. NOBODY IS EVER THAT SATISFIED, ESPECIALLY OVER AN EXTENDED PERIOD OF TIME. THE CUSTOMER IS EITHER NOT BEING CANDID, OR IS NOT BEING CONTACTED."

THEODORE LEVITT

Who bothers to complain?

Who actually picks up the phone, takes up a pen or gathers the courage to *complain?* You might think it's the trouble-maker, the difficult customer, the one who enjoys being angry. You'd be wrong.

Research shows that complaining customers are over-whelmingly loyal and sincere. They are complaining to you because they *care* about your business and about the service they receive. They intend doing business with you again in the future, and they want you to set things right.

Customers who call, write or show up in person have been *perturbed* beyond their threshold. Go beyond their threshold of pleasure and you may receive a compliment. Go beyond their threshold of pain and you trigger a complaint. The key word is *'their'*. It doesn't matter what *you* think is a reasonable waiting time, product performance, or length of warranty. What matters is what *they* expect, and whether you meet the mark.

Most people who have a gripe won't bother to complain. They'll just walk away. Therefore, each person who *does* complain represents a larger number who didn't make the effort. What's the ratio at your organization? Is it 1 out of 10? 1 out of 50? 1 out of 1,000? This means the person who complains should be *valued* that many times over! Is that how *you* treat them now?

It's true that a few odd folks will complain simply because they *enjoy* making other people squirm. They can be loud and obnoxious but offer no constructive suggestions. Even when you work hard to recover and please them they will continue to complain and moan. The truth is, they don't want to be satisfied. They enjoy being a pain in the neck.

We tend to think about these people often because they make so much noise. But the truth is they are a *tiny* percentage of your actual customer base. I call them *turkeys*. Let them gobble.

When things go wrong, use S.E.R.V.I.C.E.

S is for *say you're sorry.*

There's nothing like a sincere apology, delivered right away, to let people know you care. There's no need to grovel, nor to apologize forever. One honest and heartfelt apology will suffice.

E is for *expedite solutions.*

The faster you fix the problem, the better. This is not the time to calculate the cost of repairing the damage. Do whatever it takes to set things right. Costs will be forgotten; benefits last forever.

R is for *respond to the customer.*

Remember, real people are involved, not just products, dates and orders. Take the time to empathize with customers who have a problem.

V is for *victory to the customer.*

Build higher levels of loyalty by giving customers more than they expect. Refunds, discounts, special assistance, extra services; it doesn't have to be money. Do it fast! No loyalty is gained from a gesture that takes months to negotiate or approve.

I is for *implement improvements.*

Change your processes, systems and training to avoid the problem next time. Institutionalize hard-earned improvements.

C is for *communicate results.*

Spread the word so everyone can learn from what happened. Give full information about consequences and improvements.

E is for *extend the outcome.*

Don't stop working when they stop complaining. Stay in touch until the customer comes back and their loyalty is assured.

They bounced back!

Imagine you are going up a ski lift and accidentally drop one of your gloves or ski poles into the woods below. At **Deer Valley Ski Resort** in Utah, the staff help you find the missing item, and then give you a coupon for a free hot chocolate. Ski on!

I had a bad experience on **United Airlines** many years ago. I wrote in to complain. They sent me back a very nice letter with a fifty dollar voucher attached! Is that a crazy waste of money? Not at all. It cost me hundreds more to buy a ticket and use the voucher. Plus, they got me back on board another United flight to give the airline another chance. Today, years later, I am still a frequent flyer.

A new Italian restaurant announced their grand opening with great fanfare in the press. Every table was reserved weeks in advance. On opening night, the ovens broke down and could not be restarted!

The restaurant served an elegant buffet of cold dishes and plenty of wine. *All free!*

The next night, the ovens were back to work. Delighted customers have been going back to eat ever since!

> *"Don't lose your head when problems arise! Work with your customers to set things right."*

How generous should you be?

Victory to the customer means giving customers more than they expect. But how much should you give away when things go wrong? Just how *generous* should you be?

The answer is: *"Whatever it takes for your customer to feel you have made a genuine and generous gesture."*

This will vary depending upon how seriously your customers have been harmed or inconvenienced by your error, flaw or oversight. If a customer's shirt is burned in the laundry, that's one thing. If their entire golf course is burned by the application of too much fertilizer, that's a completely different story.

The level of repayment may also vary with the cultural background of your customers. In some parts of the world, a sincere gesture of apology is enough. In other places, more substantial compensation is required.

Occupational background can also influence a customer's perception of your efforts. Someone in Accounting may do the sums and be impressed by your returning all the profit, plus fifteen percent. Someone in Marketing may want to see a bigger splash, a more dramatic recompense.

The 'extra' you give in recovery situations need not be money, products or discounts. In some cases that would be inappropriate. Instead, give extra time, more attention, better follow-up, additional training, personal contact, a higher level of care, consideration and support.

Whoever they are, whatever you do, the final result should be loyal customers who freely proclaim: *"Wow! We got more than we expected. This organization is responsible. They really do care. We'll come back again. And we'll tell others to come here, too."*

> *"GIVING YOUR CUSTOMER A LITTLE BIT MORE IS*
> *A WINNING STRATEGY. IT DOESN'T MEAN YOU LOSE!"*

What is the lifetime value of a customer?

Instead of looking at customer value based upon each transaction, consider their value to you over a lifetime of loyal interactions.

Tom Peters, legendary management thinker and author of the *Reinventing Work* series, calculates lifetime value this way:

Let's say I make a purchase worth $100. You may regard me as a $100 customer and treat me appropriately. But if I am a regular customer, I could purchase from you once a month. That means $1,200 per year. If I become a loyal customer, I might buy from you for ten years. Now we're up to $12,000.

If my loyalty is very high, I may well recommend you to my friends. If five of them trust me and my recommendation, they could also become your loyal customers, each worth $12,000. That's $60,000. Add my $12,000 back in and you'll see me as a customer with a lifetime value of $72,000.

If you see me as worth $100 what kind of treatment will you give me? How generous will you be if something goes wrong?

But if you see me as worth $72,000, how will you treat me? How far will you go to be sure you set things right?

When things go wrong don't let your customers leak away. Research shows it costs up to six times more to get a new customer than it does to fix a problem and keep the ones you already have!

"Stop the leaks!"

Christopher Hart puts it this way: *"Recovery is a different management philosophy. This mindset can change the rules of the game. It shifts the emphasis from the cost of pleasing a customer to the value of doing so."*

When your customer is ready to *explode!*

When things go wrong, customers get upset. Sometimes they blow up in anger. Follow these five steps to sanity when *your* customer is ready to *explode!*

Let your customers blow off steam!

No one is rational when they have pent-up anger. Let your customer vent the rage and fury. Don't take it personally and don't get in the way. Just open a pathway to let off the pressure.

I recently had a problem with an express courier company. I called the company and a reasonable-sounding woman answered the telephone.

"You folks messed up!", I yelled.

"OK", she replied in a very attentive tone.

"This was a very important shipment!", I continued loudly.

"OK", she replied with concern.

"And my customer is going to be quite upset", I complained.

"OK", she replied again in a calm voice.

"Well, what are you going to do about it?", I finally asked, exhausted by my own tirade.

She paused a moment. *"OK?"*, she asked gently.

"OK", I replied, smiling at her quiet but effective approach.

Then we discussed the details needed to work out a solution.

Imagine if she had asked me for all the information right away! In my anger, it would have taken me longer to give her the details and extended my frustration. Instead, she gave me the space and time to simply 'blow off steam', not taking it personally, allowing her angry customer to settle down.

Show customers you are 'on their side'

Let customers know you are there to help, not argue, defend or disagree.

Phrases like these work well: *"Oh! I am really sorry to hear that. Can you tell me exactly what happened?"* or *"I can certainly understand your frustration. Let me be the one to help you."*

Phrases to avoid sound like these: *"I've never heard of that before. Are you sure that's what happened?"* and *"It's not our policy to do anything over the phone. You have to write, fax or come in personally."*

Some words are sure triggers for angry conversations. Avoid phrases like: *"Whose fault is this?" "Who is to blame?" "About your accusation..."* These sound like phrases from a court case, which is *not* where you want to end up!

Tell customers what you will do on their behalf

Explain what steps you will take and when you will get back in touch with the results. Thank them for giving you the opportunity to set things right.

Take fast action!

Get the problem fixed. Resolve the misunderstanding. Work inside your organization as a 'champion' for the upset customer.

When you do fix the problem, go the extra mile. Do *more* than they expect. They will remember and appreciate your efforts.

Explain how the problem has been resolved

Go back to your customers and ensure they are fully satisfied. Thank them again for allowing you to help.

Remember: an upset customer tells many people about their problem. But the same customer, when satisfied by your assistance, can be a great promoter, too. *Positive word of mouth* is precious for your business: be sure you deserve it.

Bounce back by *writing* back

Sometimes you must reply in writing to your customers' problems and complaints. When that happens, follow this ten point outline to written recovery success:

1. *Give personalized attention.* Use the customer's name, not "Dear Sir/Madam".

2. *Give positive recognition.* Show appreciation for their time, effort, communication, feedback and suggestions.

3. *Show understanding and empathy for their discomfort, displeasure or inconvenience.* Apologize sincerely and completely, once.

4. *Agree on the importance of the value dimensions they have cited in their complaint.* Don't get caught up in the details of the situation. Make the customer feel right! (See page 237.)

5. *Tell the person what your organization is doing to improve service in these specified value dimensions.* Show you are sincere about your commitment to do well in these key areas.

6. *Educate your customer.* Answer any questions about their specific situation. Provide additional, useful information.

7. *Let customers know they are sincerely valued and appreciated.* Provide assurance that their voice has been heard by others in the organization. Let them know *action* has been taken.

8. *Provide extra information, convenience, a gift or compensation.* Say '...as a gesture of goodwill' or '...as a token of our appreciation'.

9. *Thank the writer again for giving you a chance to reply.*

10. *Extend the outcome.* Look towards serving them again in the future. Build loyalty to the organization.

How to make a *wrong* customer feel *right*

What to do when a customer is just plain *wrong*? They've mixed up the facts, don't understand the policy, or have exaggerated the situation beyond all belief. *Then* what do you do?

The last thing a customer wants to hear you say is: *"You're wrong."* What they want to hear is that you understand them, appreciate them and agree with them on the *importance of the value dimensions* they have cited in their complaint.

Your customer says: *"Your staff were rude and totally unprofessional."*

You reply: *"You are right to expect courteous and professional staff."*

Your customer says: *"Your policies are rigid. Your company is so bureaucratic."*

You reply: *"I agree that we should be as flexible and user-friendly as possible. Your suggestions can really help."*

Your customer says: *"This product isn't anything like what I was promised. And your price is way too high!"*

You reply: *"I am on your side in this situation. You have a right to be satisfied by whatever you purchase from us. You deserve good value for your money. Let's review what you have purchased and see if there's a better option for you."*

Notice how your responses makes the customer feel *right*. We don't argue over the facts: rude staff, stiff policies or insufficient product features. But we do *actively agree on the importance of the value dimensions* cited in their complaints.

Let's face it – the customer is *not* always right. But customers are always important, and we can make them feel much better by *agreeing* with them on the importance of the service dimensions they identify and value.

Your service was inefficient!

Dear Mr. Anderson,

Your letter has been read by our President who has asked that I reply on her behalf.

Thank you for telling us about the problem you experienced at our new service center. I can understand your frustration from waiting 35 minutes in line and do apologize for your inconvenience.

We agree with you that efficient service is essential in today's fast-paced world, especially for our valued business customers like you.

The new service center was designed to provide customers with faster service than ever before. More counters have been installed, and improved computer systems have been developed over the past 12 months.

On the date and time mentioned in your letter, we experienced a larger surge of demand than anticipated in our initial planning. From our experience and customer feedback like yours, we have adjusted staffing levels and will have more service professionals available during the evening hours.

In addition to extended counter service, we offer 24-hour access to your account both by automated telephone response and through our secure, password-protected website. I have enclosed brochures for you about these services and invite you to explore these additional convenient options. If you have any questions, feel free to call me personally and I will be happy to assist you.

Mr. Anderson, we value your feedback very highly. The company will continue to improve to give you the quality of speed, efficiency and service you expect and deserve.

Sincerely yours,

Your staff were so rude!

Dear Mrs. Lee,

I have received your letter of March 3, which I have read with genuine concern. Please accept my sincere apology for the discomfort you experienced during your recent visit.

You are absolutely right that staff attitude is vital to success. Customers should be treated with respect at all times.

When we select new staff, we screen applicants with a profiling test to help identify those with strong service values. These values are reinforced in our orientation program and again in our ongoing customer service training courses.

The staff member you cited in your letter has been shown a copy of your letter and reminded about the utmost importance of treating our customers with courtesy at all times. This person is now undergoing additional training and will be carefully supervised to ensure his actual performance meets our high standards for customer care.

Your letter has been forwarded to our Quality Tracking Department for reference in our quarterly service index. The manager of the Department has asked me to convey his appreciation for your candor and suggestions.

As a gesture of goodwill, a bouquet of flowers and a dinner voucher for two will be delivered to your office later this week. Please accept this small gift with our sincere appreciation for your continued patronage.

Mrs. Lee, thank you again for giving us this opportunity to reply. Should you have any additional questions, feel free to contact me on my direct telephone line, indicated on the business card attached.

We look forward to seeing you again in the near future.

With best regards,

Managing customer expectations

One of the best ways to *avoid* service recovery situations is to *manage* your customer expectations from the beginning. Here are three proven ways to do it.

Clear, kept promises

Build a strong reputation for making and keeping clear promises and customers will give you plenty of leeway should things infrequently go wrong.

I fly **Singapore Airlines** regularly in First and Business Class. They take *very* good care of me as a frequent flyer. One day, on a long flight to the United States, the cabin crew informed me that my vegetarian meal was not put on the flight. They offered to combine the vegetables from two other trays and serve them to me instead. *"No problem,"* I replied, *"occasionally these things happen."*

A short time later, on a flight with another airline I was trying for the first time, they too forgot my vegetarian meal. While I accepted their apologies, I avoided that airline in the future.

What was the difference? Singapore Airlines had developed a reliable history with me, a *reputation* for delivering consistently excellent service. The one time something unusual happened and they needed to *manage my expectations*, all they had to do was explain the situation and I was ready and willing to bring those expectations down.

Pre-emptive communication

When you *know* you have a situation that could lead to customer complaints, let your customers know about it in advance, but take action to put it in the best possible light.

In one configuration of Boeing 747 aircraft, eight seats in Business Class have an aisle on one side but no window on the other. (On the other side is a wall between the seats and the galley.) Some passengers complain that *"it feels like flying in a box"*.

Airlines have responded creatively to this situation. During reservations, the seats are described and promoted as 'preferred for quiet rest and relaxation'. On the aircraft, cabin crew bring an extra blanket, pillow and eye-shades to these passengers as soon as they are seated.

The seats may have no windows, but the passengers have no expectations of them, either. The bottom line? Well-rested passengers and no complaints.

Under-promise, over-deliver

Make it a habit to promise a bit less in appropriate situations and then deliver more.

If you know it's going to take you five minutes to get something from the back room, don't tell you customer it will take *"just a minute."* Instead, let them know it could take nine or ten minutes – and then return in five. The amount of time away is the same, but the impact on your customer is completely different. In the first case you are *slow*. In the second instance you are one speedy service provider.

You can use this in your personal life, too. I do. When I travel away from home, I occasionally tell my wife that I will be arriving very late at the hotel and will only call her the following day. Of course that night, before going to sleep, I call. I usually say something like: *"I miss you so much. I couldn't bear going to sleep tonight without hearing your voice."*

Don't take this approach too far! Use it sparingly and only in appropriate situations. If you constantly under-promise, your customers will come to expect it and all the power of the technique will disappear. And if your competitors don't under-promise, but do over-deliver, your customers could disappear as well!

Build a *culture* for service recovery

Some organizations have sharpened service recovery into a potent competitive edge. They understand the technique and allocate resources to be sure they do it right.

To build a powerful culture of service recovery in *your* organization, work to score highly in each of these key areas:

1. *Senior management support.* You need vigorous endorsement of service recovery as a vital element in your overall service strategy. The top team must realize that time and money spent on recovery comes back multiplied.

2. *A comprehensive recovery plan.* This must be carefully crafted, widely communicated and well-understood. Training and systems must exist to support consistent implementation.

3. *Strong service guarantees, backed with immediate action.* Strong guarantees give customers a sense of security, and staff members a target to achieve. More on this in Chapter 16.

4. *Discovery systems that seek out and quickly identify service breakdowns.* These may be internally driven with flags, filters and alarms, or may depend upon external notification from your customers, allies and business partners.

5. *Rapid disclosure of breakdowns.* When problems are discovered, you need fast communication to all appropriate parties. Don't shoot the messenger. And don't try hiding the evidence, covering up the problem or sweeping the affair under the rug. It will come out one day to haunt you.

6. *A 'SWAT team' response* to customers' problems. Once a problem area is identified, you want tightly coordinated, dramatic action to nail those problems to the wall.

7. *Customer-effective solutions* are evaluated by your customer's perception and results, not the time, cost or effort required.

You may think you have done a wonderful job of setting things right, but if your customer is not happy and loyal, you have lost the game.

8. *Meaningful customer compensation* means giving generously to those inconvenienced by the problems. Give enough to show your sincerity and generosity.

9. *System improvements* make sure the problems won't be repeated. Lock in gains for your organization with new systems, better training and improved procedures.

10. *Reward and recognition for the team.* When a tough problem arises, the recovery team needs a pat on the back when the actions and efforts are done.

11. *Organizational learning* to capture what happened and what was done about it. Breakdowns and recoveries should be widely communicated. Lessons learned must become legends for the whole organization.

Give yourself a score in each of these eleven essential categories.

Where can *you* build a stronger culture for effective service recovery?

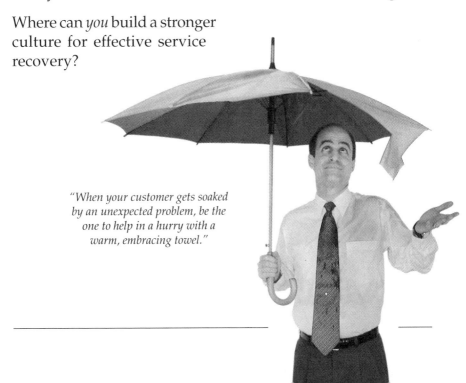

"When your customer gets soaked by an unexpected problem, be the one to help in a hurry with a warm, embracing towel."

What would *you* do?

You are the Managing Director of an express courier company. One of your trucks catches fire and the entire contents are lost. Hundreds of contracts, legal documents, bank papers and personal passports are destroyed. *What is your plan for recovery? How will you make amends with your customers? What special assistance will you provide?*

A hacker breaks into your secure server and downloads the credit card numbers of 300,000 loyal customers. *What would you say to the press? What would you say to your customers? What recovery actions would you take?*

In the coming years you will invest heavily to upgrade and improve your service. But in the short term, some customers may have expectations beyond your ability to deliver. *What conversations could you initiate with customers now to effectively manage their expectations?"*

Some upset customers scream at your staff when things go wrong. You understand how upset they can be, but you won't tolerate threats or abuse. *How can you communicate with these customers to calm them down and let them know you are doing all you can?*

"Oh boy! These are tough!"

You have a product quality problem that upsets your loyal customers. Your response was initially slow, and many customers complained. Now you understand the extent of the problem with the product and with your initial reply. *What will you do to recover goodwill with your loyal customer base?*

UP Your Service! action steps

Make a list of things that 'go wrong' for your customers on a regular basis. Make another list of the recovery steps you should take. Be sure these steps are understood by all and applied immediately.

Minimize the frequency of your customers' problems and complaints. Assemble a team of top customers and colleagues. Get answers to the following questions. What should we:
- *stop doing* that bothers our customers?
- *start doing* that our customers will appreciate?
- *do more of* to please our customers?
- *do less of* to make our customers more content?

What is the lifetime value of one good customer to you and your organization? Use the formula on page 233 to figure it out. How generous can you be to keep this customer happy? Make a list of the things you do for them when problems do arise. Are you being generous enough?

Look into your correspondence files. Pull out ten examples of written responses to customer problems and complaints. Do they measure up to the standards on pages 236–239?

There are some customers you probably should *not* serve. In my business it's those who request long proposals numerous times and never give us the job. In your case it may be those who curse and swear, or those who pay your invoices atrociously late. Instead of waiting for these customers to *become* a problem, develop a strategy to proactively remove them.

"Take action now!"

16

UP Your Service!
Guaranteed!

When customers buy from you they take on a level of risk:
risk of loss, risk of failure, risk of having made a bad choice,
risk of embarrassment or humiliation,
risk of dissatisfaction.

When you offer an UP Your Service! **guarantee**,
you remove this risk from the customer
and take it back upon yourself.

In effect, you say to your customer,
"If things don't work out the way you want, we will
do what's needed to set things right for you."

*In your customer's eyes, you become **safer** to work with,*
*more **assured**, more **confident**, more **secure**.*

And you project a better image of your organization.

After all, who would offer a guarantee if they were not
confident that most customers will be delighted?

Is this chapter worth your time to study, understand and master?
Ladies and gentlemen, I guarantee it.

What is an *UP Your Service!* guarantee?

An *UP Your Service!* guarantee is characterized by four key components. Working together, these elements give customers the desired assurance and companies the desired impact.

A clear promise of a specific outcome

You must make it completely clear *what is being guaranteed.* **Pizza Hut** guarantees lunch on your table within ten minutes of receiving your order. **Nippon Paint** promises the paint won't peel for at least five years. Singapore's **Changi International Airport** guarantees the price you pay will be no higher than prices in similar shops downtown. **Intuit** guarantees backward compatibility for their latest version of *Quicken.* Just about any measurable value dimension can be guaranteed.

In certain cases, some companies will make a *specific* guarantee of a much more *general* outcome. Rather than promising speed, durability or savings, they state: *Your Satisfaction Guaranteed.* This is a more subjective promise, but equally legitimate for the company and certainly valuable for the customer.

Reasonable conditions or even unconditional

The terms under which a guarantee is valid must be seen as fair and realistic to the customer. If you offer a guarantee and then qualify it with a range of special conditions, your customer may end up with a negative, rather than positive, impression.

For example, one European airline offered a cash-back guarantee if their flights did not leave on time. But in small print it listed conditions under which the guarantee would not apply, including delays due to weather and the requirements of air traffic control. Those two circumstances account for 97% of all flight delays!

Customers were not impressed. This guarantee generated the *wrong* kind of publicity for the airline.

By contrast, carefully study the unconditional guarantee offered by the clothing merchant **Land's End**. The elegant wording looks like this: *"Guaranteed. Period."*

Easy to file a claim and easy to collect

An *UP Your Service!* guarantee is easy for your customer to put into action. As long as the conditions (if any) are met and the guaranteed outcome is not achieved, there should be no problem at all for your customer to invoke the guarantee and collect the promised compensation.

Have a problem with your **Hewlett Packard** laser printer while under guarantee? Just call, e-mail or fax your closest Service Center and they will do the rest. No forms to fill out, no receipts to submit, no need to deal with papers.

By contrast, try getting an immediate refund at an airline counter in a foreign city for a flight you missed two weeks ago through no fault of your own. Good luck!

Meaningful and significant compensation

A strong guarantee promises action or reimbursement that more than compensates for your customer's inconvenience, loss or dissatisfaction.

The paint company will provide new paint for your building and grant another five-year extension. The pizza restaurant gives you lunch for free.

Compensation should be meaningful to the organization, too. It must be big enough to get everyone's attention. Who cares how many dissatisfied customers invoke a guarantee if there is no impact on behavior day-to-day, or on your bottom line?

Designing a valuable guarantee takes some time and deep discussion. Talk to your customers and your staff. Find out what makes a substantial difference. Then, *guarantee it*.

What are the *benefits* of a service guarantee for your *customers*?

UP Your Service! guarantees can add tremendous value for your customers and prospects.

For your new customers, an *UP Your Service!* guarantee:

- reduces the sense of risk associated with doing business with you for the first time. The existence of your guarantee sends a reassuring message: *"This company is good enough to guarantee their results. They stand behind their promise."*

- tells customers exactly what to expect. Your guarantee removes uncertainty and vagueness from a prospect's mind. This is especially useful in setting the expectations of first-time customers, expectations you can deliver upon.

- gives justification for making a choice between suppliers. If one supplier *guarantees* the work and the other says: *"Trust me, we're good at this"*, which one would *you* choose?

For your existing customers, an *UP Your Service!* guarantee:

- provides a rationale for paying premium prices and maintaining brand loyalty in the face of competition.

- makes it easy for customers to speak up on their own behalf. Many dissatisfied customers walk away, never return and never tell you why they left. A guarantee gives customers an open channel to bring their problems to your immediate attention.

- lets customers know exactly what will be done in the event of a service problem. This builds confidence, too.

- offers 'bragging rights' your customer may use in dialog with others. Having a guarantee can promote 'positive word of mouth'. The successful application of a guarantee helps avoid negative conversations.

What are the *benefits* of a service guarantee for your *employees*?

UP Your Service! guarantees also bring enormous benefits to your employees, colleagues and internal business partners.

For your employees, a strong guarantee:

- sets clear and public standards for performance. When everyone understands the company's promise, they don't waste time discussing how good is 'good enough'.

- provides an incentive to speak up about problems and seek improved solutions. This encourages all staff to accept new ideas and welcome constructive change.

- makes it easier for employees to be 'customer champions'. Guarantees reduce the tendency for upset customers to confront service personnel. Guarantees put your customers and providers *on the same side* working towards resolution.

- fosters a sense of pride about the quality of your service and the commitment of your organization.

- stimulates dialog within the organization, between shifts, departments, staff and managers at all levels.

- gives the sales team a positive differentiator to distinguish your firm from others.

"When things go wrong, the impact may be larger than you think. Should this pen company replace my pen, my shirt, or both? What would your company do?"

What are the *benefits* of a service guarantee for your *organization*?

UP Your Service! guarantees can give a terrific boost to your entire organization, clarifying objectives and aligning members of the team.

For your organization, a strong guarantee:

- requires everyone to understand and focus upon what is valuable to your customers – no sense guaranteeing a value dimension that customers don't care much about!

- forces the organization to identify problem areas and improve the service delivery process. A strong guarantee puts pressure on the organization to perform. Key points of inadequacy, failures and breakdowns surface quickly.

- communicates management's commitment to promising and achieving high levels of customer satisfaction.

- increases employee commitment, especially if you involve them in the guarantee's initial design and publicity process.

- aligns all departments towards making necessary changes and improvements. Turf wars and management silos succumb quickly to the need for coordinated action.

- formalizes your service recovery procedures. It's no longer a question of who the customer contacts or what mood your staff are in. The required action is documented and clear. After all, it's guaranteed!

- motivates the company to select, hire and train employees who will live up to guaranteed service standards.

- provides an incontrovertible way to evaluate performance, linking service provided to recorded incidents of customer dissatisfaction. Guarantees set unmistakable standards that are monitored and reported by your customers.

- gives you an objective way to tie staff and company performance to appraisals, promotions, incentives and bonus payments.

- substantiates your claim to industry leadership and competitive advantage. This is especially so if your guarantee is *first* in the market, *unique* from other providers, or features a *big payout* with substantial perceived risk for the guarantor.

- gives you a justifiable rationale for continued premium pricing of your services.

- contributes to strong brand identity and perceived customer value.

- encourages customers to speak positively about you when things don't go wrong – and when they do!

- lets business partners know what standards you expect and encourages them to cooperate on new initiatives.

- motivates internal departments to create service guarantees for other parts of the organization. This promotes a *virtuous cycle* in which everyone listens and works together to improve the quality of internal and external service.

- *increases your costs* in the short term through guarantee design, system improvements, required payouts and increased staff training, but *increases your profits* thereafter through elimination of similar problems, increased customer loyalty, enhanced brand image, continued premium pricing and greater market share.

What a service guarantee *cannot* do

Despite all the benefits, *don't launch a guarantee* if your company or department is in total disarray, has fundamental systems out of whack, is suffering from system overload or is totally dependent upon external suppliers. A powerful promise to customers won't solve these core internal problems.

Sixteen steps to launch your guarantee

1. Establish a task force to research and design the guarantee. Include managers with authority, power and resources. Include employees who will administer and be responsible for fulfilling the guarantee. Include customers, ideally those who are loyal as well as those who have *already left you* for another service provider.

2. Gather information about your customers' experiences, expectations and most important value dimensions.

3. Assess current performance levels in the industry and in your company. Where is your customers' satisfaction now at risk? Where are they most disappointed?

4. What guaranteed level of performance would produce a *significant positive impact* in your customers' perception of your organization? What would give you a distinct competitive advantage?

5. Decide *what* to guarantee. Will you guarantee comprehensive customer satisfaction, or specific performance levels for clearly identified value dimensions?

6. Evaluate your internal capabilities. How close are you to achieving the guaranteed levels?

7. Agree upon either fixed or variable payouts for the guarantee. Be sure your compensation is meaningful and has an impact on your customers and your organization.

8. Establish procedures to invoke and collect on the guarantee. *Keep it fast and user-friendly!* Make it easy for staff to help the customer. A slow response triggers customer suspicion.

9. Confirm guarantee funding and prepare additional recovery efforts. Do a 'dry run' on all procedures to ensure that the guarantee invocation won't produce another set of problems!

10. Announce the impending guarantee to your employees and relevant suppliers.

11. Create training programs to educate staff in the purpose, conditions and procedures associated with your guarantee.

12. Conduct a 'soft launch' with a selected group of customers. Monitor the program carefully and vigorously improve internal systems to meet your guaranteed standards.

13. Link your guarantee to appraisals, staff compensation and promotions.

14. Launch your guarantee to all external customers. Leverage your advantage with public relations and promotions.

15. Track results over time. Use examples of further internal improvements to build momentum and success.

16. Monitor your competitor's response. When necessary, raise the bar and guarantee a new and higher standard.

When should you launch your guarantee?

Some companies wait until they are already 100% perfect before launching a service guarantee. The trouble is, they never get around to it or, by the time they do, it's much too late – everyone else is already doing it. Their guarantee looks like a reactive 'me, too' effort.

Instead of waiting, launch your service guarantee *early* to drive improvements forward quickly. Of course you must have confidence that your team can focus on the process and live up to the promise.

Experiments show that a public guarantee (and the temporary pain of the accompanying payoffs) galvanizes staff to achieve promised goals in less time than anyone imagined.

What would *you* do?

Research shows that most customers don't cheat on guarantees. Those that do have a very low and temporary affiliation with your company, are extraordinarily upset by your past service, or are amongst the few genuine scoundrels seeking to take advantage. Your research identifies four customers you suspect of cheating, but you are not sure which category applies. *What would you do in this situation?*

A frozen yogurt shop posts a sign near the cash register: *"Your yogurt is free if our staff fail to smile and say thank you." What are the problems with this 'guarantee'? How would you revise it?*

Your market share has been declining for 12 months. A survey finds that your competitors have taken the lead with strong and well-executed guarantees. You are now preparing to launch an equivalent guarantee, even though your operations are not quite up to par. You must design a training program to educate and motivate your staff. *What will you tell them about the guarantee? How will you prepare them for the many changes this new program will require?*

You are creating a new guarantee to accompany your latest service offer. You have excellent support from the top, and staff members who are motivated to help. Your most loyal customers are keen to participate. But you also want ideas from customers you have lost over the years, those who have left you for others. *How will you ask for their input and participation? Would you offer an incentive for their help?*

"If you guarantee it, they will appreciate it... and appreciate you, too!"

UP Your Service! action steps

Make a list of ten value dimensions your customers seek when they buy or do business with you. Which of these key areas do you *guarantee*? Would you gain competitive advantage by offering a guarantee in the others?

Identify one functional area of your current operations that is problematic or undeveloped. If you were to improve dramatically in this area, what new promise could you make to your customers?

Now conduct a bold experiment. Announce to a select group of good customers that you will *guarantee* a higher level of performance in this functional area for a trial period of six months, beginning in one month's time.

Give the undeveloped department full management support and watch for astounding results. Then extend the experiment to other divisions and departments.

Surf the Web to seven different sites that offer commercial transactions on-line: airline tickets, automobiles, books, music, playground equipment, video recorders and vitamins. Print out the *'Satisfaction Guaranteed'* statement from each site. Compare them and select the policy or wording that gives you the greatest sense of confidence and reassurance. Compare those statements with the guarantee on your organization's website. Do what's necessary to make yours one of the best.

"Go! Go! Go! Go!"

"It's a funny thing about life; if you refuse to accept anything but the best, you very often get it."

W. SOMERSET MAUGHAM

17

UP Your Service!
Integration
and Innovation

You serve great coffee. But that's all you serve.
You won't be in business very long.

You offer the same products as everyone else, but they take orders
over the telephone, by fax and on the Internet.
You provide only face-to-face service at your storefront.
Your storefront's days are likely numbered.

You make alliances with others to sell
their products and services with yours,
creating one point of contact for your customers.
You are on the road to greater glories.

You push the envelope in speed, variety and convenience,
giving shoppers new and more reasons to buy from you.
They will.

Which way are you going?

Are you inventing, combining and advancing towards the future?
Or are you destined to be a relic of the past?

Merge two or more fields

Developing new service ideas can be as simple as merging two different fields to create an innovative and integrated offer.

Combine a bookstore with a coffeeshop (**Borders** does it very well). Put a tailor on an aircraft (**Virgin** does on flights to Hong Kong). Mix a children's playground with a family lunch (you'll find it at **McDonald's**). Unite a computer with a telephone, an alarm clock and a camera (**Nokia** will offer you the latest). Blend senior citizen housing with healthcare (**Marriott International** has a division specializing in life-care communities).

Merge driving with banking, eating with entertainment, cooking with learning, and shopping with gasoline, museums or laser eye surgery in the mall! Mix anything with anything and you have the potential for an innovative, integrated service.

But don't count on your customers to tell you what they want! No one asked **Jeff Bezos** for an all encompassing website offering books, toys, electronics, drugs, travel, collectibles, auctions, finance and more. But his vision for **Amazon.com** is to mix it *all* together!

No one asked **Akio Morita** to put a tape deck in our pockets, but the **Sony** *Walkman* he invented changed our expectations and our lives.

What can *you* combine with *your* service to give your customers something new, something fresh, something special?

> "KEEP ON GOING AND THE CHANCES ARE
> YOU WILL STUMBLE ON SOMETHING,
> PERHAPS WHEN YOU ARE LEAST EXPECTING IT.
> I HAVE NEVER HEARD OF ANYONE STUMBLING ON
> SOMETHING SITTING DOWN."
> CHARLES F. KETTERING

Integrating for customers on the inside...

One sure-fire way to make your service more valuable to your customers is to *do more work for them* inside your organization. Rather than asking them to contact one department for sales, another for shipping details, a third for questions about finance and yet another for customer service, provide a *single point of contact* for all communications and solutions.

This 'one face to the customer' requires an effective organizational structure plus cross-training and collaboration between departments. Rotate staff from one department to another. This boosts understanding and leads to improvements.

Locate staff from different sections of the company into a common area. **Stephen Ng** did this when he launched the *Customer Responsiveness Center* for **Motorola** in Hong Kong. Instead of being across town, representatives from various divisions were now across the room. Communication improved right away. Service to customers did, too.

...and on the outside

Don't stop tying things together inside your organization. Reach out to other vendors, suppliers and agencies. Do all you can to handle the details on your customers' behalf.

The City of Sunderland arranges utilities for companies who lease out factory space. At the Prime Minister's Office in Singapore is a special division called **Contact Singapore**. Their primary purpose is to help people with talent get involved with this small and highly motivated country. They will assist you with information and contacts for education, housing, leisure, company registration, immigration, investment funding and employment of qualified staff – even schooling for your children! Check it out on-line at **www.ContactSingapore.org.sg**

Turn negatives into positives!

Another way to innovate is to take something customers like least and generate new ways to add more value.

At **Raffles Hotel**, four rooms are a bit smaller than all the others. Naturally they tended to be sold last and were less popular with the guests. The General Manager, **Jennie Chua,** took a completely different view. She invested in fine artworks and hung them attractively on the walls. Renamed *'The Gallery Suites'*, these rooms now sell very quickly and at a higher price!

Seats in the balcony at a theater in London sold slowly and at a very low price. The manager changed that entirely by making the balcony an innovative *event*. Before the show, a few cast members mix with the audience, only in the balcony. An extra snack bar is set up to avoid lines during intermission, only in the balcony. The performers make strong eye contact during the performance and at the end of the show..especially with those in the balcony. The manager raised the price of the now popular balcony tickets. Profits increased by 10%!

No one enjoys walking home from shopping in the rain. **Ikea** offers huge umbrellas at just $3.00 each on a rainy day. But if the sun is shining the cost is a full $10.00!

Giordano lets you *rent* an umbrella at a very low price and get your money back after the storm! They don't mind if you keep it, either. It's good advertising for the store and a memorable instance of *UP Your Service!* especially for you.

I've been vegetarian for years. At lunch or dinner, colleagues often worry if I'll find anything good to eat. No problem! I ask the waiter to tell the chef about a special guest who wants a *spectacular vegetarian surprise.* I give no further instructions about ingredients or cooking style. I haven't been disappointed yet!

"IN ADVERSITY LIES THE SEED OF INNOVATION."

Leverage any value dimension

Take any value dimension and stretch it to the limits. You will find a whole new realm for exciting service innovations.

One hotel in New York prides itself on *personalized service* for an exclusive clientele. The laundry department is a case in point. They keep track of client preferences for starch, folding and hangers, and they also do much more. The department:

- buys matching buttons for all their clients' clothing. When a button is missing, they replace it,

- has a tailor on staff to maintain cuffs, hems, pleats and buttonholes in like-new condition,

- knows when each guest is checking out and carefully launders and packs the wardrobe for departure,

- maintains a storage facility for any clothing their guests will not need until their return to New York City,

- diplomatically monitors the condition of all clothing. When a piece approaches the end of its better days, they take a digital picture of the article and send it by e-mail to selected fashion houses and designers. These trusted partners send back swatches of similar fabric with sketches of new designs for guests to consider.

Does this extra service cost more? Of course. Are guests willing to pay the price? Absolutely. And this is just the laundry! Imagine what they do in catering and reception.

Fuji Xerox is developing a hassle-free photocopy machine. Don't wait until your copies look bad to call the Service Center. And don't pay for regularly scheduled maintenance calls you may not need. Instead, buy a machine with a telephone line and diagnostic software pre-installed. When your photocopier needs to be serviced, the machine will call Fuji Xerox and make an appointment by itself! That's *leveraged* maintenance value.

What would *you* do?

Streamline, Inc. does shopping, errands and deliveries. They install a custom-designed refrigeration unit in your garage, and you give them access with a key. All the items in your kitchen and pantry are scanned into their web-based ordering system. Need more of anything at all? Click for it on the website and it's delivered the following day. Want it automatically restocked? They can do that, too. Ready for a picnic? Just choose the style and an entire basket will be pre-loaded and delivered. Streamline promises convenience and an additional 3–5 hours of time for you each week. New customers actually move into neighborhoods they serve just to enjoy the service. *How can you become every bit as valuable to your customers? What can you do to innovate and integrate your service?*

You have been hired by a local business community to help increase retail sales. On one side of the main street are a food market, a bookstore and a restaurant. Customers flow freely from one outlet to another, but when it rains, traffic to all three precipitously declines. You see an opportunity to add value for customers by tying these outlets together with cookbooks, classes, weekly recipes, specially packaged grocery bundles, coordinated restaurant menus and convenient home delivery. *How would you design this unique collaboration? How would you promote it? What role would each outlet play to maximize revenues and customer interaction?*

"UP Your Service INSIGHTS" is the second book in the UP Your Service series. It's packed with stories, examples and good ideas – including many from readers like you!

Order your copy today (see page 296) and send in your best ideas for the *next* book to NewIdeas@RonKaufman.com

UP Your Service! action steps

Make a list of three things your customers dislike, avoid or complain about. Gather your most creative people and host a brainstorming session. *How can you take a different approach to these areas of customer frustration? How can you turn the adversity to your advantage?*

The digital world brings speed, accuracy and instant recall to data. Identify three areas where you are still bounded by paper records, physical systems and off-line processing. What electronic innovation would accelerate your service and minimize your mistakes? Take your thinking forward to develop proposals and plans, and then implement them.

Make a list of all the things your customers must *do* in order to explore, secure, receive, enjoy and fully benefit from your service. Who must they speak to? Who do they need to call? What forms will they fill out? What documents or information must they submit? Where do they go? What time do they need to be there? What do they need to bring along or take back with them later? *How many of those things can you do for your customers so they don't have to do it for themselves?*

What business are you in? Go to the *Yellow Pages* and select fifteen totally unrelated businesses. For each one, make up at least one way you could 'merge' your offering with theirs to create a totally unique and innovative offer. Nothing is too outrageous to consider.

The world is full of outrageous ideas that make a lot of sense...like committing yourself to a partner, creating a loving family and living your lives in joy. Cheers to you!

"Let's go faster!"

18

Keeping Track of Service

You pour money and attention into an aspect of your business.
Has it made your service better?

There are fewer customer complaints than before.
Has your service actually improved,
or have your customers given up?

Your competition claims they give 'the best service in town'.
You are not so sure. Can you prove it?

Your quality improvement team wants to work
on one specific aspect of the business.
Which one would you ask them to attack?

These questions need well-grounded answers
to keep your company moving forward.

You can't just fly by gut-feel and the seat of your pants.

You need to track how you are doing
and in which direction you are headed.

You need to ask your customers a series of
useful and productive questions.
You need input, ideas and opinions.

You need to read this chapter.

Measurements can be complex

Developing a sophisticated customer service tracking system can become a formidable project. Taken to extremes, a comprehensive program could include compiling an index, using cluster, stratification, conjoint, regression and variance analyses, and looking at extrapolation curves, sigma deviation charts and much more.

All of these *quantitative* approaches can help you analyze your customers and your business. And, they can take a substantial amount of time, money and expertise. If your business warrants such detailed investigation, by all means contact a specialist in your area and get to work.

But tracking service performance can also be direct and simple. The questions in this chapter will not generate exhaustive quantitative detail, but they will provide valuable *qualitative* insights you can act upon to *UP Your Service!* right away.

Measurements can be straightforward

Many satisfaction surveys feature long lists of multiple choice questions, asking customers to check little boxes and tell the company whether they:

- *are completely unsatisfied, very unsatisfied, unsatisfied, somewhat satisfied, satisfied, very satisfied or completely satisfied.*

- *strongly disagree, disagree, are neutral, agree, or strongly agree.*

I find these questionnaires boring and potentially misleading. Answering so many repetitive questions often causes my mood to drift lower, affecting my replies. Furthermore, my *'somewhat satisfied'* and your *'satisfied'* may be exactly the same, or possibly worlds apart.

There is another approach: **KISS** – *Keep it simple, smartie!*

Track customer expectations

Find out why customers choose you in the first place and what they **expect** an *UP Your Service!* provider like you to deliver. You can modify these questions to fit your culture and your customers. Ask them in person, over the telephone or in writing.

- *"**Why** did you select our organization to serve you?"*

- *"We'd like to know what is genuinely **important** to you. What are the top five aspects of our service that matter to you most? For example, is it speed, accuracy, staff attitude, comfort, price? There are many other areas, as well. Which ones matter most to you?"* (Note: this question highlights your customer's top-rated value dimensions.)

- *"Please help me **prioritize** the elements you have just listed. Amongst them which are most important, least important, and which are in the middle?"*

- *"In your opinion, what **must** an excellent service provider do for you? What do you consider absolutely essential for a company to earn your business?"* (Note: this gives you an idea of the 'satisfiers' your customers insist upon.)

- *"And what, if anything, must an excellent service provider **never do** if they want to keep your business?"* (Note: this gives you an understanding of the 'dissatisfiers' that could drive your customers away.)

- *"Over time, many things will change. As we grow into the **future**, what do you expect from us? What service would you expect us to provide more of? Is there anything you expect us to do less of? Are there services you expect us to start providing? Is there anything you expect us to stop doing?"*

Stay ahead of the curve. Ask these questions often and watch for anomalies or trends in your customers' replies.

Track customer perceptions

Once you understand what customers expect, the next step is to find out how well they think you are doing. What are their **perceptions** of your current service?

- *"Let's look at each of the areas you said were very important. How well would you say we are doing right now? Are we doing better than you expected, close to what you expected or not as well as you expected?"*

- *"If you said we are doing better than you expected, what exactly are we doing that you appreciate, enjoy or find useful?"*

- *"If you said we are not doing as well as you expected, in what way is our performance not up to your standards or expectations?"*

These questions help you track service quality from your customers' point of view. Asking regularly helps you observe general trends, for better or for worse, in your delivery and customer satisfaction.

"How does your service measure up?"

Track customer preferences

If you are going to make improvements, expand your line of products or change your service in any way, it's good to know in advance what changes your customers would **prefer**.

"If we could change two or three things to make our service to you even better than it is right now, what would you like us to do? Of your suggestions, which should we do first?"

Track competitive position

Want to know how well you are doing compared to the competition? Ask your customers!

- *"Have you worked with other service providers in our industry? Do you notice differences between their service and ours?"*

- *"Is there anything other service providers are doing you would like us to consider doing, too? Is there anything they are doing you would like us to definitely avoid?"*

- *"Relative to other players in the industry, would you say we are improving our position, staying about the same, or slipping behind?"*

Who are you going to ask?

In addition to *what* you ask, *who* you ask will determine the quality of answers and ideas you receive. Don't restrict yourself to a random sampling of current customers. You can dig deeper to uncover greater value. Question your:

- *prospects,* those who have not yet chosen you, to help reveal your competitive position.

- *first-time customers,* those who are new to your organization and will bring a fresh perspective. They can help you assess current buying trends and changes in expectations.

- *loyal customers,* your long-standing patrons, who will let you know what you are doing well and what you must continue to improve.

- *former customers,* those you have lost, who will put you in close touch with where you are weak and must improve.

- *staff and service partners*; the questions in this chapter can help fine-tune internal service, too.

What would *you* do?

Dell Computer measures their customers' experience every day. They keep close track of three key areas: order fulfillment, product performance and service-and-support. In each area, Dell focuses on one metric above all others. For order fulfillment they follow 'ship to target': how often a completely correct order gets to the right customer on time. For product performance they track 'initial field-incident rate': how often something goes wrong with a new computer once it has been delivered. For service-and-support they note how many times a service technician corrects a customer's problem on-time and in just one visit.

What key areas are most important to your customers? Which metrics would you follow to track your performance in each?

Incidentally, Dell aims to improve each of these measurements by fifteen percent per year. And they succeed. Can you?

You are preparing a customer satisfaction survey and want to contact a group of your competition's customers. Some advisors in your company feel this is neither ethical nor productive. They say, *"Let's focus on who we have already and how to keep them."*

"Use a well-designed survey to get inside your customer's head!"

What do you think? What is your reply?

UP Your Service! action steps

Contact three market research companies. Ask for information about the methodologies they use to measure customer satisfaction. Study the results they offer and the benefits they can bring to your investigation: specialized expertise, rigorous approach, computer tabulated results and more.

Study the customer satisfaction surveys used by other organizations inside and outside your industry. Which do you admire? Which do you call into question? Why?

Select a team of outgoing staff to survey your customers. Add people from Marketing, Sales, Operations and Customer Service to the team. Working with the ideas in this chapter, have them develop a set of questions to ask your customers. Decide which customers to ask. Decide whether to ask in person, over the telephone or in writing. Go out and conduct the survey.

Pass the results of your survey to another cross-functional team. Have them study the data and brainstorm a wide array of ideas and possible action steps to address your customers' interests, hopes and concerns.

Decide which ideas and action steps to implement first. Communicate throughout your organization which actions will be taken, and why. Then, implement the selected actions.

Six months later, repeat the process. Assess the impact of your actions and determine what to work on next. Repeat the cycle again, and again, and again.

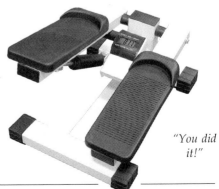

"You did it!"

19

What Wise People
Say About Service

We are graced with the gift of language.
The words we use bring our world into being.

We have the power to invent or destroy,
encourage or degrade, inspire and uplift,
motivate, captivate or humiliate
ourselves and those around us.

The choice is entirely ours.

Focus on what you do not enjoy
and you'll have more of it to suffer.

Talk about the good things in life
and more good things will come to you.

"ARGUE FOR YOUR LIMITATIONS, AND SURE ENOUGH, THEY'RE YOURS."
RICHARD BACH

"COMMON SENSE IS INSTINCT. ENOUGH OF IT IS GENIUS."
GEORGE BERNARD SHAW

"PEOPLE WHO SERVE AND FEEL GOOD,
AND THOSE WHO ARE SERVED AND FEEL GOOD,
DON'T GO TO WAR."

ARTHUR KAUFMAN

"CONSCIOUSLY OR UNCONSCIOUSLY,
EVERY ONE OF US DOES RENDER SOME SERVICE OR OTHER.
IF WE CULTIVATE THE HABIT OF DOING THIS SERVICE DELIBERATELY,
OUR DESIRE FOR SERVICE WILL STEADILY GROW STRONGER
AND WE WILL MAKE NOT ONLY OUR OWN HAPPINESS,
BUT THAT OF THE WORLD."

MAHATMA GANDHI

"WHEN THE ALARM BELL RINGS, YOU'D BETTER WAKE UP
AND REALIZE THAT THE CUSTOMER EXPECTS MORE
FROM YOU TODAY THAN HE DID THE DAY BEFORE.
YOU'D BETTER FIND WAYS TO BE BETTER."

GARY TOOKER

"THE PRINCIPLE WAS RIGHT THERE
— YOU COULDN'T MISS IT.
THE MORE WE DID FOR OUR CUSTOMERS,
THE MORE THEY DID FOR US."

DEBBI FIELDS

*"Above all be of single aim;
have a legitimate and useful purpose,
and devote yourself unreservedly to it."*

JAMES ALLEN

*"No company has a permanent consumer franchise.
No one has the only game in town.
The never-ending cycle of destruction and change
inherent in a capitalist economy always provides
new opportunities for those with
determination, goals and concentration."*

HARVEY MACKAY

*"It is well worth remembering that the customer
is the most important factor in any business.
If you don't think so, try getting along
without him for a while."*

NAPOLEON HILL

*"After-sales service is more important
than assistance before sales.
It is through such service that
one gets permanent customers."*

KONOSUKE MATSUSHITA

"THERE IS LITTLE DIFFERENCE IN PEOPLE,
BUT THAT DIFFERENCE MAKES A BIG DIFFERENCE.
THE LITTLE DIFFERENCE IS ATTITUDE.
THE BIG DIFFERENCE IS WHETHER
IT IS POSITIVE OR NEGATIVE."

W. CLEMENT STONE

"QUALITY IN A SERVICE OR PRODUCT
IS NOT WHAT YOU PUT INTO IT.
IT'S WHAT THE CLIENT OR CUSTOMER
GETS OUT OF IT."

PETER DRUCKER

"BE A GOOD LISTENER.
YOUR EARS WILL NEVER GET YOU IN TROUBLE."

FRANK TYGER

"ONE HUNDRED MINUS ONE CAN'T BE NINETY-NINE
IN THE HOTEL BUSINESS. IT MAY BE ZERO.
IF ONE EMPLOYEE OUT OF HUNDREDS GIVES A
BAD IMPRESSION TO A CERTAIN CUSTOMER,
IT WILL BE ONE HUNDRED PERCENT DAMAGE FOR
OUR HOTEL IMAGE FOR THAT CUSTOMER."

ICHIRO INUMARU

"The purpose of life is not to win.
The purpose of life is to grow and to share.
When you come to look back
on all that you have done in life,
you will get more satisfaction from the pleasure
you have brought into other people's lives
than you will from the times that you
outdid and defeated them."

HAROLD KUSHNER

"We make a living from what we get.
We make a life from what we give."

SIR WINSTON CHURCHILL

"When a child is born, it cries and the world rejoices.
Live your life so that when you die,
the world will cry and you will rejoice."

INDIAN SAYING

"If the person you are talking to
doesn't appear to be listening, be patient.
It may simply be that he has
a small piece of fluff in his ear."

WINNIE THE POOH

*"THE MORE WE GIVE OF ANYTHING,
THE MORE WE SHALL GET BACK."*

GRACE SPEARE

*"TEACHERS OPEN THE DOOR,
BUT YOU MUST ENTER BY YOURSELF."*

CHINESE PROVERB

*"KNOWING IS NOT ENOUGH;
WE MUST APPLY.
WILLING IS NOT ENOUGH;
WE MUST DO."*

GOETHE

*"THE BEST WAY TO FIND YOURSELF IS TO
LOSE YOURSELF IN THE SERVICE OF OTHERS."*

MAHATMA GANDHI

"I AM A PENCIL IN THE HAND OF GOD."

MOTHER TERESA

"You can never learn less.
You can only learn more."

R. BUCKMINSTER FULLER

"Never look down on anybody
unless you're helping him up."

THE REVEREND JESSE JACKSON

"Do all the good you can,
by all the means you can,
in all the ways you can,
as long as ever you can."

JOHN WESLEY

"Life is a big canvas,
throw all the paint on it you can."

DANNY KAYE

"Be outrageous.
It's the only place that isn't crowded!"

AUTHOR UNKNOWN,

BUT RON KAUFMAN AGREES

"WE LIVE IN AN EXTRAORDINARY TIME.

AT A RATE UNPRECENDENTED IN HUMAN HISTORY,
POLITICAL, SOCIAL AND BUSINESS INSTITUTIONS
ARE UNDERGOING RADICAL CHANGE.

NATIONS, IDEOLOGIES, ORGANIZATIONS AND EVEN FAMILIES
ARE REINTERPRETING THEIR MOST BASIC DECLARATIONS
AND ARTICULATIONS OF THEIR CONCERNS.

IN THE MIDST OF THIS DYNAMIC WORLD, WE SEE
THE EMERGENCE OF A NEW PARADIGM;
ONE THAT RECOGNIZES OUR RELATIONSHIP
WITH LANGUAGE AS THE PLACE IN WHICH
INNOVATION AND POETRY OCCUR.

FOR THIS WE NEED TO LEARN TO ACCEPT
OUR HUMAN FATE AND, AT THE SAME TIME,
BE RESPONSIBLE FOR OUR INTENTIONS AND PLANS,
LISTENING SENSITIVELY TO FIND
WISDOM AT THE CROSSROADS.

IN THIS NEW PARADIGM WE CAN BE DESIGNERS
OF A FUTURE IN WHICH PEACE, WEALTH,
JUSTICE AND COMMUNITY CAN FLOURISH.

LET US DESIGN THIS WORLD TOGETHER."

DR. FERNANDO FLORES

TO COMMEMORATE GRADUATION FROM THE
ONTOLOGICAL DESIGN COURSE,
APRIL 1993, BERKELEY, CALIFORNIA

What do *you* have to say about service?

We are coming to the end of a book, but the beginning of an *UP Your Service!* journey.

The opportunity to share and apply the ideas you have learned rests within your hands.

What you do now will make your customers more contented, your colleagues more inspired, your business more successful, your family more loving and your chosen communities more intimately woven.

What will you say to those you care about? What will you do for those you serve? How will you express your dedication to continually *UP Your Service?*

My words to you are those of thanks: for your time within these pages and your interest in the ideas we have explored.

As you put these ideas into action you will earn success and a service reputation. You will discover challenges, too. Keep going, keep learning, keep moving forward. Carry on in your caring for others and serving those around you.

The world will respond to your efforts with grace, gratitude and good fortune.

I would be pleased to meet you one day, face to face, to share a moment or two of mutual delight and admiration.

May you be inspired and delighted daily.

"LET'S MAKE THIS DANCE UPON THE EARTH THE BEST THAT IT CAN BE.
IT'S UP TO US TOGETHER NOW. LIFE RESPONDS TO YOU AND ME."

RON KAUFMAN

20

Inspired Acts of Service

*What is providing **UP Your Service!** really all about?*

Is it the pursuit of profit, the desire for gain and the endless quest for competitive advantage?

These are valid reasons to serve and serve well, but they are not the only motivations.

Giving UP Your Service! to others also brings something precious and deeply personal back to you. It may be fulfillment or pleasure, or a sense of intimacy or achievement.

When you look back at your life and consider all you've said and done, what will you remember most fondly?

Will it be the sales you made and the profits you earned, or all moments when you assisted others and they reached out to help you?

"WE ARE ALL ANGELS WITH ONLY ONE WING. WE CAN FLY ONLY BY EMBRACING EACH OTHER."
LUCIANO DE CRESCENZO

Brighten up those around you

Selfless service brightens up your life and illuminates those around you. Here are just a few great ways to do it:

- **Volunteer** at a school, old-age or childrens' home, hospital, soup kitchen, crisis hotline or other community organization.

- **Clean up a mess** you did not make in a park, at the beach, by the road, around the neighborhood or on a wooded trail.

- **Donate** items of value to a charity. Give away your extra clothing, furniture, food, cars or money.

- **Bake cookies** or buy your favorite sweets. Give them away to co-workers, colleagues, neighbors, police officers, bus drivers and those working 24-hour shifts at the fire station.

- **Give compliments** to those you meet, serve and work with. Tell others how good they look or how pleased you are to see them. Write notes. Leave uplifting voicemail messages. Be sincere. Be special. Be in service.

- **Pay the charge** for another person. Buy their movie ticket, pay their highway toll, cover the cost of their lunch. Don't stick around for their gratitude in person. Let their surprise be your reward.

What is your most inspired act of service? Send me a note. I'd be glad to know!

"Celebrate the miracle of life!
May yours be long and successful,
with good health, good friends
and much love."

Organ donation is a final act of service

When it's time to go (and may that time be long and far away), you may wonder if there is one more gesture you can make in service to another human being. Is there one final act of contribution to enrich the life of an individual or a family?

The answer is 'yes'. You do have one more precious option.

Signing an organ donor form enrolls you in a worldwide program to give the gift of life to others. It means that your vital organs, including your kidneys, liver, heart, eyes or other healthy tissues can be given to another person so that they may continue to live and love and serve.

What a remarkable feeling to know that the blessing of health is carried on from you to others. What an extraordinary way to add precious value even after you are gone. What a miraculous gift to give to individuals and their family members.

Becoming an organ donor is easy: you simply complete and sign a form with two witnesses and submit it to your local Department of Health or other appropriate agency. You will receive an organ donor card to carry in your purse or wallet.

This is a very personal issue. I deeply respect your personal thoughts and feelings, and your decision. If this is a gesture you feel is right for you, take the simple steps to make it happen. Give the gift of life as your final act of service on the Earth.

For information about organ donation in Singapore, visit: **http://www.thegift.org.sg** or e-mail to **thegift@nkfs.org**

For organ donor information in the **United States**, contact: **http://www.organdonor.gov**

For information in other parts of the world, contact your local hospital, Department of Health or other appropriate agency.

A

action steps, 15, 27, 41, 69, 87, 97, 115, 131, 145, 161, 173, 189, 205, 223, 245, 257, 265, 273
Adia Personnel Services, 164
advertising 119
after-sales service, 103, 136
airline service, 10–11, 93, 123, 240–241, 248
    see also airline company names
Allen, James, 277
Amazon.com, 92, 106–107, 179, 260
American Express, 35, 159, 165
Amway, 202
Andersen Consulting, 21, 38
anniversaries, 198, 216
Apple Computer, 201
Archimedes, 49
Asia Pacific Breweries, 62
Aspen Mountain Ski Area, 185
AutoDesk, 221
Avis Rent-a-Car, 164

B

Bach, Richard, 275
Bakers Dozen, The, 19
Barbie doll, 177
Barrie, Sir James M., 25
BBC, 185
benchmarking, 37, 106–107, 159, 161
Best of Active Learning, The, 187
Bezos, Jeff, 260
Bible, The, 45
Big Mac, 32
Blanchard, Ken, 22
BMW, 203
body language, 210–211
Body Shop, The, 19, 202
Borders (bookshop), 260
British Airways, 24
buddy, 48, 51
Burger King, 33

C

'can-do' spirit, 21
Cap Gemini Ernst & Young, 38
Carlzon, Jan, 118
Cartier, 178
Celestial Seasonings, 200
Changi International Airport, 57, 248
Chaplin, Charlie, 167
Charles Schwab, 220

child-care, 57
children's perception, 127, 138
Christie's, 203
Chua, Jennie, 262
Churchill, Sir Winston, 279
Cisco Systems, 46
Citibank, 38
City of Sunderland, 261
CNBC, 185
CNN, 199
Comfort Taxi, 19
communication
    bulletin boards, 222
    internal, 55
    spoken, 212–215, 234–235
    written, 216–217, 236
    see also body language, e-mail, telephone, voicemail
community relations, 62, 67
company history, 34, 196
compassion, 20
compliments, 12, 209, 219
computer upgrades, 109
Contact Singapore, 261
continuous improvement, 22, 37
    see also service
Corporate Image Management, 194
courier service, 125
    see also courier company names
Crescenzo, Luciano de, 285
customer
    complaints, 156, 226–229, 234–235, 238–239
    compliments, 157
    contact, 147–161, 207–223
    empathy with, 24
    expectations, 10, 240–241, 270
    feedback, 24, 36, 147–151, 228, 261, 267, 272
    lifetime value, 35, 233, 245
    loyalty, 4, 8–9, 168
    perceptions of, 250, 270
    profile, 149
    relationships, 71
    responding to, 230–234, 235–237
    surveys, 150, 267–273
    types, 8–9
    understanding, 147–149
    value, 2
    see also communication, telephone, value dimensions
Customer Contact Corporation, 154
customer information database, 35
Customer Responsiveness Center, 261

D

data, *see* information
Deer Valley (ski resort), 231
delivery systems, 31, 71
Dell Computer, 10, 202, 272
dentist, pediatric, 126–127
DHL (courier), 92
Disney Interactive, 178
Disneyland, 94
Domino's Pizza, 31
Drucker, Peter, 278

E

e-business, 87, 172
e-commerce, 172, 179
Einstein, Albert, 39
e-mail, 218–219
   signature file, 223
eBay (auctions), 90
empathy, 24
ERA Realty, 183
Erhard, Werner, 209

F

family, 12, 264
Famous Amos, 121
Federal Express (courier), 92, 159
Fidelity Investments, 220
Fields, Debbi, 276
Flores, Dr. Fernando, 282
FMC, 23
focus groups, 81, 115, 158
Forbes, Malcolm, 226
Ford, Henry, 227
Formula One, 159
Four Seasons Hotel, 36
Frequently Asked Questions (FAQ), 204,
   220
Fuji Xerox, 263
Fuller, R. Buckminster, 281

G

Gandhi, Mahatma, 276, 280
Gardner, Ava, 167
Gate Gourmet, 183
General Electric, 169
General Mills, 169
General Motors, 165
generosity, 18–19, 209, 232, 286
Giordano, 34, 262
Globe Silk Store, 20
Goethe, Johann Wolfgang von, 280

Government of Singapore, 38
   see also Contact Singapore
Grand Historic Hotel (training program),
   167
Gretzky, Wayne, 171
guarantees, 247–257
   benefits of, 250–253,
   compensation, 249
   designing, 254–255
   unconditional, 248–249

H

Häagen-Dazs, 177
Hall of Fame, 48, 59
Hargrove, Michael, 225
Harrods, 155
Hart, Christopher, 233
Heathrow Airport, 24
Hewlett Packard, 50, 249
Hill, Napoleon, 277
Hope, Bob, 187
Howard, Steven, 194

I

IBM, 60
Ikea, 159, 262
information, 191–205
   and service cycle, 199
   mandatory, 201
innovation, 259, 260, 262, 264
insurance, 110–111
integration, 259–265
Intel, 58, 178, 204
internal service partners, 195
Internet, 31, 46, 87, 199
   see also websites
Intranet, 61
Intuit, 37, 248
Inumaru, Ichiro, 278

J

Jackson, Michael, 167
Jackson, The Reverend Jesse, 281
Jaguar, 203
joint-venture partners, 197
Jollibee Restaurants, 22

K

Kaufman, Arthur, 276
Kaye, Danny, 281
Kennedy, John, F., 165
Kettering, Charles, F., 260

Kipling, Rudyard, 167
Kushner, Harold, 279

L

Land's End (clothing retailer), 34, 249
Lapidus, Todd, 154
Le Meridien Hotel, 150
Le Meridien Hotel (Dubai), 80
Levitt, Theodore, 228
Lion City, The
   see Singapore
lines, 184–185
Linux, 203
Lion King, The, 178
listening posts
   see customer feedback
logistics, 102

M

Mackay Envelope, 149
Mackay, Harvey, 149, 277
Macy's, 155
Malcolm Baldridge Award for Quality, 159,
   168
management
   and staff, 56
   role modelling, 63
   see also organization structure
Manulife, 58
Many Memorable Experiences (training
   program), 167
market share, 168
Marriott Hotel, 165
Marriott International, 260
Mary Kay Cosmetics, 202
Massachusetts Institute of Technology, 56
MasterCard, 95
Matsushita, 63
Matsushita, Konosuke, 277
Mattel, 177
Maugham, W. Somerset, 167, 257
McDonald, Ronald, 32
McDonald's, 32, 260
MGM Grand Hotel, 186
Michener, James A., 167
Microsoft, 59, 207
mirroring and matching
   see body language
mission statement
   see service vision
Moment of Truth (questionnaire), 150

Moments of Truth (book), 118
moments of truth
   see perception points
Morita, Akio, 260
Mother Teresa, 172, 280
Motley Fool, The, 164, 202
Motorola, 37, 168, 180, 261
Motorola University, 51
Mr. Bean, 185
mystery shopper, 154

N

NASA, 165
National Eye Centre (Singapore), 58
National Library Board (Singapore) 170,
Neurolinguistic Programming (NLP), 210,
   211
Ng, Stephen, 261
Nike, 21
Nippon Paint, 248
Nissan Motors, 61
Nokia, 260
Nordstrom, 91
Novell, 46

O

OCBC Bank, 51
One Minute Manager, The, 22
One World, 93
one-shot deal, 89, 90, 94
Orchard Dental Centre, 126
organ donation, 287
organization
   culture, 59, 252–253, 261
   environment, 57–58, 69, 118
   management, 56
   operations, 102
   pledge, 60
   structure, 38, 53
Otis Elevator, 185
Outlook, 227

P

packaging, 119, 178
Pentium (computer chip), 204
perception points, 91, 117–131, 175–189
   and service cycle, 122–125, 129
   auditory, 120, 181
   gustatory, 121, 183
   kinesthetic, 120, 182
   olfactory, 120, 183
   visual, 120, 180
Peters, Tom, 233

Philips, 58
Pizza Hut, 159, 248
Pocahontas, 178
policies
    user-friendly, 33–34, 119, 179–180
    plain language, 180
Porsche, 57
powerful partnerships, 89, 93, 95
products
    quality of, 30, 118
    perception of, 177
protocols, 216–217
provenance, 203
Prudential Assurance, 45, 159, 180

Q

queues
    see lines
questions, 208
quick-fixes, 61
Quicken (software), 37, 248
quiz, 3, 5

R

Radio Shack
    see Tandy Corporation
Raffles Hotel, 166–167, 262
Raffles International, 167
Raffles, Sir Stamford, 166
Rainbow Room (New York), 181
Reinventing Work (program), 233
reliable relationships, 89, 92, 95
Ritz Carlton Hotel, 64, 141, 173
Robbins, Anthony, 211
role play, 50
Rolex, 177

S

SAS Institute, 57
SATS, 59
Scandinavian Airlines, 118
screensaver, 169
senses
    see perception
service
    and products, 6–7
    and relationships, 12
    basic, 74–75
    benefits for business, 4
    benefits for customers, 2–3
    code of conduct, 27
    competition, 155
    criminal, 72–73

culture, 43–69, 72, 242–243
cycles, 99–115, 129, 142, 199, 219
desired, 78–79
expected, 76–77
interactions, 89–97
mindset, 17–27
recovery, 225–245
scenarios, 14
skills, 50
speed of, 187
standards, 6–7, 71–87, 115
surprising, 80–81
toolset, 29–42
types of, 2–4, 72–83
unbelievable, 82–83
values, 167
vision, 44–45, 68, 69, 163–173, 198
24-7-365, 198, 222
    see also action steps
Service Quality Centre, 64, 173
Shangri-La Hotel, 159
shareholders, 197
Shaw, George Bernard, 275
Sheraton Towers (hotel), 95
Silicon Harbor (Hong Kong), 180
Singapore Airlines, 52, 150, 176, 227, 240
Singapore Girl, 176
Singapore Press Holdings, 48
Singtel Mobile, 183
Six Sigma (program), 168
Sony, 30, 60, 260
Sotheby's, 203
Southwest Airlines, 46, 159
Speare, Grace, 280
Squaw Valley, 202
staff
    appraisals and promotions, 53
    attitude, 139, 142
    empowerment, 64
    generosity, 18–19
    motivating, 165, 251
    orientation, 47–49, 69
    perception of, 118, 130, 176
    recruitment, 46, 69, 100, 112
    responsibility, 23
    rewards and recognition, 52, 53
    social events, 54
    suggestion schemes, 61
    training, 22, 32, 50–51
    see also continuous improvement
Standard Chartered Bank, 60
Star Alliance, 93
Starbucks, 121
Stew Leonard's, 121, 198
Stone, W. Clement, 278

Streamline, Inc., 264
suppliers, 197
*Swim With the Sharks Without Being
    Eaten Alive*, 149
Swissair, 11, 183
Switzerland, 11

T

10X (program), 168
Tandy Corporation, 165
Tax Authority, 186
teambuilding, 26
telephone
    hotline, 151, 228
    protocols, 212–213
    service on, 119
    see also voicemail
Texas Instruments, 47
Thurber, Marshall, 117
Tiffany's, 178
Tiger (beer), 62
TNT (courier), 92
Tooker, Gary, 276
Top Box Quality (program), 168
Total Customer Satisfaction (program), 37
Tower Records, 120
tracking
    see customer surveys
traditions, 59
transaction satisfaction, 89, 91, 94
trust, 34, 113
Tyger, Frank, 278

U

U-Haul, 200
United Airlines, 91, 120, 150, 231
United Artists Theaters, 58
UP Your Service!
    rationale, 1
    see also service, continuous
        improvement
UPS (courier), 92
user's guide, 78
user-friendly,
    see policies
user-to-user, 10

V

value dimensions, 133–145, 164
    and service cycle, 142–143, 145
    assessing, 154–155
    common, 139
    hard, 134–135

leveraging, 263
personal, 140–141
soft, 136–137
value-added, 56, 140
Versace, 120
video feedback booth
    see customer feedback
viewpoints, 56
Virgin Airlines, 120, 260
virtuous circle, 253
vision
    see service vision
voicemail, 55, 214–215, 222, 224

W

Walesa, Lech, 65
Walkman, 260
Wall of Fame, 27
Wall Street Journal, The, 141
Walt Disney World, 94
Web, The
    see World Wide Web
website, 36, 119, 124, 200, 220–222
weddings, 176
    planning, 106
Wesley, John, 281
What would *you* do?, 14, 26, 40, 68, 86,
    96, 114, 130, 144, 160, 172, 188,
    204, 222, 244, 256, 264, 272
Winnie the Pooh, 279
work stations, 57
World of Sports, 52
World Wide Web, 10, 40, 41, 220
www.barnesandnoble.com, 172
www.ContactSingapore.org.sg, 261
www.coolsigs.com, 223, 225
www.organdonor.gov, 287
www.thegift.org.sg, 287

Y

Yellow Pages, 87, 265

UP Your Service! training programs

Everything you need in complete learning systems to get your service and your customers' loyalty going *UP!* Featuring Ron Kaufman in professionally produced video and audio. Easy-to-use and proven worldwide. *Backed by Ron's 100%, no-risk, money-back guarantee.* To order now, see page 297.

The Secrets of Superior Service

Eight steps to achieve superior service:
- Fly over rising expectations
- Excellent service mindset
- Improving service standards
- Managing customer expectations
- Bounce back with service recovery
- Appreciate complaining customers
- Take personal responsibility
- See the world from your customer's point of view.

High-impact for frontline staff, supervisors and managers. Three hours on video and audio, including posters of key learning points, trainer's discussion guide and workbook.

ISBN 981-00-8946-5

Partnership Power!

How to build progressive and proactive partnerships inside and outside your organization. Best practices in the service cycle of *explore, agree, deliver* and *assure.*

Excellent for deepening relationships with your customers and suppliers, colleagues, distributors and other partners. These principles make sense in your personal life, too!

More than two hours on video and audio, plus complete viewer's guide with key learning points.   ISBN 981-04-1787-X

Service Encounters of the Third Kind

Shift your focus from simple 'transaction satisfaction' to creating profitable, long-term 'customer loyalty'. Discover the shifts you and your team must make in training, mindset, focus and goals.

Essential education for supervisors and management teams. The future is determined by the actions you take today. This shows you what to do! One hour on video and audio with viewer's guide. ISBN 981-00-8948-1

Quality Service *LIVE!*

One of Ron's hottest presentations with a LIVE audience of 3,000 screaming fans. World-class education *and* motivation in a one-hour video that gets you pumped up and ready to *serve*. Terrific for team or staff meetings and fast training programs. ISBN 981-04-1661-X

Ron Kaufman is... *Unbelievable!*

Break through the glass ceiling to reach the very *top* and achieve your highest goals. Profit from this LIVE inspirational speech for an audience of 2,000 insurance agents in Singapore. Tailored for the industry and the local audience. One hour of fast-action ideas, insights and humor. ISBN 981-00-8949-X

Your no-risk, money-back, rock-solid GUARANTEE.

Your investment in these active learning programs is *100% guaranteed*. Use them for 90 days. If you are not completely satisfied with the impact on your people and your service, return for a complete refund.

www.RonKaufman.com